WORLDS OF TRUTH

WORLDS OF TRUTH

A Philosophy of Knowledge

Israel Scheffler

A John Wiley & Sons, Ltd., Publication

This edition first published 2009
© 2009 Israel Scheffler

Blackwell Publishing was acquired by John Wiley & Sons in February 2007. Blackwell's publishing program has been merged with Wiley's global Scientific, Technical, and Medical business to form Wiley-Blackwell.

Registered Office
John Wiley & Sons Ltd, The Atrium, Southern Gate, Chichester, West Sussex, PO19 8SQ, United Kingdom

Editorial Offices
350 Main Street, Malden, MA 02148-5020, USA
9600 Garsington Road, Oxford, OX4 2DQ, UK
The Atrium, Southern Gate, Chichester, West Sussex, PO19 8SQ, UK

For details of our global editorial offices, for customer services, and for information about how to apply for permission to reuse the copyright material in this book please see our website at www.wiley.com/wiley-blackwell.

The right of Israel Scheffler to be identified as the author of this work has been asserted in accordance with the Copyright, Designs and Patents Act 1988.

Library of Congress Cataloging-in-Publication Data

Scheffler, Israel.
  Worlds of truth : a philosophy of knowledge / by Israel Scheffler.
      p. cm.
  Includes bibliographical references and index.
  ISBN 978-1-4051-9170-8 (hardcover : alk. paper)
  1. Knowledge, Theory of.   I. Title.
  BD161.S325 2009
  121–dc22

                              2008053935

A catalogue record for this book is available from the British Library.

Set in 10.5 on 13pt Minion by SNP Best-set Typesetter Ltd., Hong Kong
Printed and bound in Malaysia by Vivar Printing Sdn Bhd

01   2009

Contents

Preface   viii
Acknowledgments   x

Introduction   1

Part I: Inquiry   5

Chapter 1: Justification   7
  1. Beliefs   7
  2. Access to truth   8
  3. Cogito ergo sum   9
  4. Mathematical certainty   11
  5. Classical logic   12
  6. C. I. Lewis' empiricism   14
  7. Access as a metaphor   17
  8. J. F. Fries and K. Popper   18
  9. Voluntarism and linearity   19
 10. One-way justification   20
 11. Beginning in the middle   21
 12. Justification, contextual and comparative   22
 13. Justification in the empirical sciences   23
 14. Circularity versus linearity   25
 15. Democratic controls   25
 16. Interactionism   27

Chapter 2: Truth   30
  1. Allergy to absolute truth   31
  2. Provisionality and truth   32

3. Truth versus verification   34
4. Truth and fixity   36
5. Transparency, Tarski, and Carnap   38
6. Truth and certainty   42
7. Sentences as truth candidates   44
8. Theoretical terms   44
9. Varieties of instrumentalism   45
10. Pragmatism and instrumentalism   45
11. Systems, simplicity, reduction   46
12. Crises in science   51
13. Reduction and expansion   52

Chapter 3: Worlds   **55**
1. Philosophies of truth   55
2. Operationism and truth   57
3. Version-dependence   59
4. Differences among scientifically oriented philosophers   61
5. Monism, pluralism, plurealism   62
6. Realism versus irrealism   66
7. A theory of everything   72
8. The status of ethics   75
9. Emotive theories; Ayer and Stevenson   75
10. Moore's ethical intuitionism   77
11. Dewey and ethical naturalism   79
12. Symbol, reference, and ritual   81

Part II: Related Pragmatic Themes   **93**

Chapter 4: Belief and Method   **95**
Introduction   95
1. Problems of pragmatism and pragmatic responses   98
2. Peirce's theory of belief, doubt, and inquiry   102
3. Peirce's comparison of methods   104
4. Difficulties in Peirce's treatment   106
5. An epistemological interpretation   108
6. The primacy of method   109

Chapter 5: Action and Commitment   **114**

Chapter 6: Emotion and Cognition   **125**
  1. Emotions in the service of cognition   126
  2. Cognitive emotions   132

Index   143

Preface

This work is not a textbook but a treatise, explaining and building on my work in different areas of philosophy over the past half century. I have wanted, in this book, to accomplish two main purposes: first, to draw attention to the common themes and organizing emphases implicit in the analyses I have undertaken, in this way providing a sense of my philosophical directions throughout, and second, to affirm certain new convictions to which they have led me.

To this end, I have had perforce to restate and often to reformulate several of my prior results, fitting them into a general framework along with new analyses, to articulate the philosophical pattern which characterizes my views. I hope the reader will forgive such necessary repetitions, bearing in mind the larger context they are meant to serve here.

My book thus gives a sense of my organizing themes and also offers an account of fundamental conclusions to which my recent thinking has driven me, my epistemological sympathies being pragmatic, my methodological practice analytic. The result is an overview of my philosophy of knowledge, encompassing an approach to aspects of epistemology, of truth, and of metaphysics. The following paragraphs explain the structure of the whole.

The Introduction provides an overall sketch of my philosophical orientation.

The main part of the book (Part I) is divided into three chapters, the first devoted to the topic of *justification*, the second to the topic of *truth*, and the last to the topic of *worlds*. Three succeeding chapters (Part II) illustrate and elaborate the treatment of certain central themes of the book.

The first main chapter, "Justification" (Chapter 1), addresses epistemological issues, concerning how truths are chosen. Here I argue against linear approaches to justification and advocate interactionism instead, an approach in which the warrant of our assertions is diffused throughout the whole mass of our beliefs rather than concentrated in a single locus thought to be guaranteed by certainty or decided by fiat.

The second, "Truth" (Chapter 2), offers a transition from epistemology to reference, passing from a concern with how truths are acquired to what they affirm: Here, I take up the cudgels for absolute truth, a presently unpopular notion mistakenly thought to have been displaced by science and overcome by verificationism or deconstruction. I firmly disentangle absolute truth from absolutism, emphasizing linguistic and systematic relativity, and eschewing certainty.

The third, "Worlds" (Chapter 3), deals with metaphysical topics. Here I consider philosophical debates between monists and versional pluralists, and, rejecting both these schools of thought, I come out in favor of what I designate as plurealism, the doctrine that there are many real worlds—not either none, as irrealism claims, or exactly one, as physicalists claim. We live, I hold, in several worlds, made known to us through scientific methods, yielding a variety of truth clusters not reducible to one. A theory of everything is a fairy tale mirage, science having two moments, the one reductive, pursuing economy, the other expansive, ever seeking new realms to explore and cultivate.

Part II of the book, "Related Pragmatic Themes," rounds out the portrait of my philosophy of knowledge.

Chapter 4 relates my pragmatic orientation to its classical source in Peirce, emphasizing his critique of Descartes, his anti-foundationalism, and his understanding of science.

Chapter 5 offers one attempt to apply my interactional view of justification not only to science but also to ethics.

Chapter 6 relates understanding to the emotions, whether in science, philosophy, or art, thus exemplifying the pragmatic emphasis on connecting theory and practice.

Acknowledgments

The scholarly debts I have incurred over the past half century are beyond enumeration. I must, however, here express my enduring gratitude to philosophical teachers from whom I have learned, and continue to learn— to Nelson Goodman, Sidney Hook, Ernest Nagel, C. G. Hempel, W. V. Quine, and Morton White—as well as to colleagues and friends who have furthered my education to the present day—to Catherine Z. Elgin, Sidney Morgenbesser, Hilary Putnam, Robert Schwartz, David Sidorsky, and Harvey Siegel.

I am fortunate to have spent five decades of my academic career at Harvard, as a Professor of Philosophy and Education, and the last five years at Brandeis, as Scholar-in-Residence at the Mandel Center for Studies in Jewish Education, both institutions having provided me with unparalleled intellectual environments, unstinting support, and warm colleagueship.

For assistance in preparing my manuscript, I have had the superb help, at Brandeis, of Emmajoy Shulman-Kumin and Valorie Kopp-Aharonov, the former in the initial stages and the latter in the concluding stages of the work. Earlier phases of portions of the manuscript profited from the excellent assistance of JoAnne Sorabella of the Harvard Graduate School of Education.

Finally, I offer my sincere thanks to the following publishers for permission to reprint the papers presented in Chapters 4–6: to Stauffenburg Verlag, to the Journal of Philosophy, Inc., and to the Teachers College Record at Columbia University; as well as to Mouton de Gruyter, a Division of Walter de Gruyter & Co. KG Publishers, for permission to use certain passages in Part I, Chapter 3, section 12.

Introduction

Inquiry, in every case, reaches out to the new; the quest for certainty is the quest for an end to inquiry.* Rejecting this quest shapes a distinctive epistemological attitude—one that is prominent in the pages to follow. Such attitude, increasingly prevalent in much recent thought, has, however, also been typically partial, marking off one or another favored realm, notably that of meaning, science, ethics, or philosophy, where certainty continues to hold sway. I here adopt no such favoritism.

In related nominalistic spirit, I reject reliance on presumed necessities, whether natural or linguistic, as fundamentally unclear, and I abjure the notions of analyticity and synonymy as well. Accordingly, the quest for a certainty based upon meaning is abandoned.[1]

Nor is there any room for certainty in my conception of science, often claimed to rest on a hard core of the sensory given. Evidence, argument, test, and probability are obvious touchstones in science, but none is founded on an array of immutable sensory judgments. Although observation may indeed dislodge theory, theory may also overrule observation, and one observation may conflict with another. Observation relates to theory not as the certain to the probable but rather as the particular to the general. Clashing with theory, an independently credible observation report may provoke a re-equilibration of belief, but the resulting system may as well exclude as well as include such reports.

The foundational view of knowledge as a superstructure reared upon a rock-solid base is thus opposed, along with the obverse doctrine of pure coherence. If science is not an airy fantasy, neither is it an edifice resting upon basic beliefs beyond the threat of change. A better image of science

* This introduction draws upon my *Inquiries* (Indianapolis: Hackett Publishing, 1986), xi–xiii.

is that suggested by Charles Sanders Peirce, of a cable made of many inter-woven fibers and stronger than any of these, none of which is indispens-able. Alternatively, a more recent suggestion of Karl R. Popper compares science to a house built on stilts over a swamp, and Otto Neurath likens science to a ship being continually rebuilt upon the open sea. To analyze the anti-foundational spirit of science while affirming its credibility is the task of scientific justification in my view.[2]

Because the pattern of such justification applies not only to science but also to ethics, I grant no safe haven for certainty in the latter realm either. No act or belief is an island. Each has systematic ramifications. Each can survive only within a changing community of surrounding acts or beliefs, whose claims demand equal consideration even if they do not uniformly carry equal weight. Such a picture does not, of course, imply that no act or belief is durable or stable. It implies only that stability is not a self-evident privilege or entitlement but rather an achievement, to be reconciled with the demands of continuing systematization.

The epistemological attitude I have characterized extends also to phi-losophy, which, no more than the realms of meaning, science, or ethics, gives sanctuary to certainty. Philosophy has no direct access to higher reali-ties, firmer principles, or keener insights than are available elsewhere. As I view it, philosophy is systematic interpretation and deliberation. Reflecting upon prior belief and practice, it analyzes, questions, criticizes, and sys-tematizes, thus modifying the initial objects of its attention.

It begins, not at the beginning with a clean slate, but in the middle and after the fact. As Peirce put it in his critique of Descartes' method, "We cannot begin with complete doubt. We must begin with all the prejudices which we actually have when we enter upon the study of philosophy."[3] Whatever illumination philosophy may yield is an outcome of its work upon such prejudices rather than a consequence of its transcendent cer-tainties projected upon a vacant field.

Philosophy stands, not outside the sphere of common thought and experience but squarely within it. It carries no epistemological immunity to the common ills and distempers of inquiry. Logic, evidence, clarity, system, truth—all make their demands of philosophy no less than of other domains of the intellect and, where philosophers fall short, they can offer no special excuse. What is distinctive about philosophy is not its certainty but its comprehensive curiosity, not its infallibility but its interest in under-standing every sphere of thought and life. If philosophy is not self-sufficient, however, neither is it powerless. It presupposes, but also reworks, the pre-philosophical matter from which it sets out. Like science, from which it cannot be sharply distinguished, it may yield novelty and reveal the unseen.

Like science too, it is pluralistic, and in three main senses. First, its problems are plural, drawn from any region whatever of human interest or conviction. Second, its concepts are not pre-ordained; they need to be devised or chosen out of an infinite array of alternatives. Third, its solutions are not uniquely related to the problems they address. For any systematic interpretation preserving the preferred truths of some object domain, there will be incompatible others that do the same. Yet, to provide *any* adequate interpretation, in philosophy no less than in science, is a significant feat; pluralism is not nihilism. An adequate interpretation is a triumph of insight and order available to all—hence an instance of intellectual progress.

Such progress of the understanding is not limited in its import to the understanding. It colors our feelings, memories, perceptions, anticipations, and actions. Philosophy is no more a spectator sport than is science or art. Its analyses modify habits; its techniques channel visions; its visions organize sentiments and orient conduct. Such connectivity of theory and practice, affirmed by pragmatism, rings true to me and inclines me toward that philosophy—in its broad outlines at least, and despite my criticisms, elsewhere, of certain of its specific formulations.

There are, of course, variant readings of pragmatism, as of every philosophical movement, and some are too soft for my taste. That philosophy is social does not mean it is merely social; that it comments on culture does not imply it is only cultural commentary. Philosophy converses, but is not swallowed up in conversation. If its starting points are not fixed and its paths and destinations are plural, yet it traverses a hard terrain imposing a severe discipline. No more than science can it simply will its conclusions. No less than science does it strive for objectivity relative to independent constraints, variable as these may be. Objectivity without certainty, relativity but not subjectivism, truth consistent with pluralism—these are the pragmatic emphases I admire.

It follows that I see no rift between pragmatism and analytic methods in philosophy. Without argument and analysis, pragmatism is mere attitude, not philosophy proper. As I read the great American pragmatists, they came not to bury philosophical analysis but to apply it to novel effect over a wide range of contemporary problems. Nor can current analyses, of whatever school, be enclosed within a small circle of technical concerns.

There can in fact be no conflict between range and argument, between vision and technique. This conviction, at any rate, has helped sustain the variety of my philosophical efforts over the years.

These efforts have addressed problems in different sectors of philosophy but they evince certain common methodological features. My preference for meager means in logic and ontology is motivated not by miserliness but by the consideration that philosophical obscurity as well as triviality of result both tend to increase with metaphysical extravagance, and the further consideration that a solution gained under methodological constraints is likely to survive their relaxation, but one achieved in their absence will not generally outlive their imposition.

The logical attitude pervading my work is, accordingly, minimalist, an attitude I learned from my teacher, Nelson Goodman, who, while severely restricting his logical apparatus, radically expanded the range of his philosophical endeavors to embrace not only science but also art, not only the literal but also the metaphorical, not only cognition but also emotion, not only denotation but also exemplification and expression.[4]

Notes

1   For detail, see my *Beyond the Letter* (London: Routledge & Kegan Paul, 1979), pp. 7ff. and 132, nn. 10–12.
2   Israel Scheffler, *Four Pragmatists: A Critical Introduction to Peirce, James, Mead and Dewey* (London: Routledge & Kegan Paul, 1974), pp. 54, 56–57. See also Chapter 4 in this volume.
3   Ibid., pp. 52–53; see also Charles S. Peirce, *Collected Papers of Charles Sanders Peirce*, Charles Hartshorne and Paul Weiss, eds. (Cambridge, MA: Harvard University Press), vol. 5.
4   Nelson Goodman, *Languages of Art*, 2nd ed. (Indianapolis: Hackett Publishing, 1976).

Part I
Inquiry

Chapter 1

Justification

1. Beliefs

I have cited, with approval, Peirce's doctrine that we begin to philosophize not in a state of complete doubt but rather possessed of minds stocked with all sorts of beliefs. We cannot divest ourselves of these at one stroke and wipe our slates clean, any more than we can jump out of our skins with a single leap. Our fate is to begin our thinking careers not at the hypothetical beginning but in the middle of things.

We find further that, from the very earliest acknowledgment of our thoughts and opinions, we are more strongly attracted to some rather than to others, inclined to consider the former more persuasive or initially credible than the latter. When such differences become objects of continuing reflection, stimulating alterations in the relative attractiveness of our beliefs, we have, in effect, turned critical without deliberate effort. Our initial mass of beliefs, layered from the start by our attitudes toward their claims, is subject to altered layering, progressively filtering out beliefs we find inconsistent or otherwise repugnant and assigning the rest the credentials corresponding to their respective current attractiveness. These credentials are not fixed once and for all; they arise, change, and grow as we ourselves continue to grow. Our beliefs, in sum, are persuasive not because of their provenance but because of their up-to-date credentials. Pedigrees count for nothing.

Our beliefs are, if persuasive, not so simply because of what they individually assert. They of course purport to be true but their respective claims need to survive the challenge of living within a community of comparable claims, each demanding equal consideration and the combination threatening potential conflict and modification. In short, each of our beliefs requires amicable relations with our other beliefs to nourish its credibility.

2. Access to Truth

A stronger moral has often been drawn from this situation: No belief, it has been roundly declared, has direct access to truth, but only indirect access at best, thus giving rise to unavoidable reliance on justification by supporting evidence.

A representative statement is that of Bonjour, "If truth were somehow immediately and unproblematically accessible ... so that one could in all cases opt simply to believe the truth, then the concept of justification would be of little significance and would play no independent role in cognition. But this epistemically ideal situation is quite obviously not the one in which we find ourselves. We have no such immediate and unproblematic access to truth, and it is for this reason that justification comes into the picture."[1]

Here, however, looms a problem. If a belief acquires indirect access to truth only through its justification by others supplying evidence for it, these others must themselves be justified; they cannot simply be plucked out of the air. But since they themselves have no more direct access to truth than the belief they purport to justify, they must be justified in turn by still other beliefs, and so on *ad infinitum*—unless the justification chain can be safely brought to a halt. Without such a halt, no belief can have any access to truth, lacking direct access by hypothesis, and incapable of gaining indirect access as we have seen.

Clearly, the last link in our hypothetical chain cannot be justified by the first link, on pain of vicious circularity, the whole circle then afloat aimlessly with no firm anchorage anywhere. The most widespread solution proposed by many thinkers, early and late, is to deny the initial supposition that no belief has direct access to truth, and to affirm that at least the first link in a justification chain is indeed certain, having direct access to truth, which truth it channels to subsequent links, thereby assuring them access that is indirect. The picture is familiar in the history of philosophy, in association with both rationalist and empiricist thinkers, the former grounding supposed initial links in reason, rendering them impervious to doubt, the latter basing the certainty of such links on a presumably hard core of sensory data given in experience. Both schools of thought accordingly suppose that the vast array of items we take to be true gain their credibility through evidential chains linking them ultimately to beliefs true beyond doubt.

The flaw in this solution, from a contemporary point of view if not from that of the historical masters, is its appeal to the notion of truths transparently beyond the possibility of doubt. The intervening centuries have disappointed us so often in the claims to such truths as to render us immune to their deceptive charms. Again and again, impregnable claims of self-evidence have been not only doubted but roundly defeated, in mathematics as well as the empirical sciences. An initial sketch of the general picture reveals that mathematics—the home of rationalistic philosophy—far from being a haven of unquestionable truth, thrives on doubt, speculation, and conjecture. Empirical science—the inspiration of empiricist thought—in its turn, has repeatedly spawned new credible theories baffling to the dogmatisms inherited from prior science.

3. Cogito Ergo Sum

We consider now Descartes' celebrated rationalist gem, the thought, "Cogito ergo sum" (I think therefore I am), which he deemed to show his own existence incapable of being defeated by the most radical doubt, even by a hypothetical malicious demon bent on deceiving him into doubting his own existence.[2] For to be deceived is to be; to doubt that I exist is itself to think, hence to be. Here, then, for Descartes, is a truth he is compelled by reason to accept and barred by reason from doubting—and each of us who considers the equivalent statement in reference to himself must reach the equivalent and certain conclusion. We have, then, in every such case, a proposition absolutely incapable of being doubted, by its author at least, if not by others. And there's the rub.

For if I, the author of the statement, "Cogito ergo sum," am prevented from doubting it, others are free to dispute it without hindrance. An outside observer might well have reason to doubt, of the utterer of a particular "Cogito"-statement, that he had in fact been thinking while mouthing the words "I think," as against the possibility that the words were not deliberate but merely thoughtless reflexes, or unthinking products of someone brain dead, even in fact dead, during the time in question.

If actually brain dead during the critical interval and revived only afterward, the utterer might at first affirm that he had been conscious continuously, and deliberate throughout the relevant interval, later admitting the critical gap in his thinking when confronted with outside evidence. The "Cogito" utterance in question here was, then, false, hence not beyond doubt.

It has been argued, in rebuttal, that the "Cogito" utterance might have been doubted by others but not, however, by the author himself *at the time of the utterance*, even were he to doubt its veracity at a later time. In reply to this rebuttal, it might be insisted that the proposition itself was, at any rate, subject to doubt hence not certain, as shown by the reasons later available to both author and outsider. Nevertheless, proponents of the rebuttal would persist in arguing that while both author and outsider might be able to detail these reasons for doubting the phrase, the author alone could do so *only after the fact*. Unlike the outsider, he could not very well credit these same negative reasons at the very moment of his utterance, thus denying while affirming it in the same breath. Hence, this argument triumphantly concludes, the phrase "I think" was certain and beyond doubt for the utterer himself at the critical moment of its enunciation even though such certainty were to evaporate a moment later.

The argument is, however, confused, since if the utterer acquires good reasons to retract his vulnerable utterance at a later time, it had evidently been vulnerable from the start, hence not beyond doubt even then. The utterance, therefore, cannot well be judged to have been certain even for the utterer and even at the critical time of its origination. Were the mere impossibility of affirming and denying a statement at the same time to imply that it was certain, every statement whatever would be certain.

Is it not, however, strange that first-person cases differ from third-person cases with respect to the notion of evidence? We may query the doctor who has just examined a patient to detail his evidence for thinking the patient is feeling sad or for its seeming to him that the sky is growing darker, but we would not demand of the patient himself who has just said "I'm feeling sad" or "It seems to me the sky is growing darker" that he outline his supporting evidence for these judgments before we credit him with knowing, even granting the truth of these claims. Some have accordingly argued that there is no logical room for the concept of evidence about one's own case, which implies that the utterer's statement is certain for him at the time of its enunciation.

There is nothing, however. to prevent the patient himself from offering the very same reasons as those offered by the doctor. It is not that there is no logical room for the concept of evidence in one's own case, but that we do not require the utterer to supply such evidence before judging him to know what he claims, by his affirmation, to know, if we take it to be indeed true. We normally grant that the utterer is in a favored position to judge his own case without recourse to the evidence needed by the outsider, his affirmation assumed to be highly credible to him, if not to us, in consequence of his favored position. Nor do we make this typical assumption only with respect to a subject's report of his phenomenal experiences. If he tells us his name, we do not, barring special circumstances, query him as to his evidence, nor do we quiz him for his reasons if, looking out the window, he tells us that a snowstorm is raging outside.

It is, however, important to note that, in assuming high *prima facie* credibility of certain self-referential assertions, for the subject at least, we are not excluding the possibility of error. A man may be mistaken about his pains or moods or even his own name. We are nevertheless allowing a subject's favored position in certain self-referential cases to give him the right to affirm his belief short of an actual or presumed evidential argument. If we also judge his belief to be true, we may then decide that he indeed knows what it affirms. But infallibility is in any case out of the question, as both he and we may be mistaken, having good reason to retract our claims in the future.[3]

4. Mathematical Certainty

Is there not then, as many suppose, a basis for certainty in the realm of mathematics? Much depends on the particular interpretation given to mathematics. Modern thinkers have typically distinguished between uninterpreted and interpreted formal systems. Euclidean geometry, for example, when uninterpreted, rests on undefined primitive terms assigned no denotations and on postulates relating these terms selectively to one another, with rules governing the formation of sentences and the creation of defined terms, as well as approved ways of moving from certain sentences to others. With no denotative import, however, uninterpreted sentences are not truth vehicles at all, having the status of abstract structures only, similar to games. None is therefore, *a fortiori*, true beyond doubt.

Interpreted through the assignment of suitable denotations, however, the sentences of the formal geometrical system do become truth vehicles, but they become vulnerable thereby to doubt and rejection. When Euclidean points are, for example, taken to denote stars and Euclidean lines to denote light rays, the resulting assertions, purporting to be physically true, become hostages to physical evidence which may controvert them, hence to disconfirmation.

What about pure mathematics, free of special postulates and popularly thought to be transparently true in itself? Part of the current popularity of this opinion rests on the belief that mathematics has been reduced to logic, the firmest of truths, as presumably shown by Whitehead's and Russell's *Principia Mathematica*. Sadly, however, the purported reduction has been demonstrated to proceed not all the way to logic, but only to logic plus (interpreted) set theory, while set theory itself is plagued with paradoxes, alternative incompatible foundations, controversial existential assumptions, and metaphysical differences, hardly the stuff of self-evident truths.[4]

5. Classical Logic

What then about classical logic, that is, the logic of sentences as well as of quantification and identity? Surely, this is so firm that it is clearly not subject to doubt. The problem that arises from an English speaker's claiming to have doubted, and indeed to have rejected, a logical truth, by saying, "not (not (p and not-p))," is that he has made his claim utterly incomprehensible to native English speakers; they would incline to take him as a non-English speaker or, at any rate, as not using the word "not" in conformity with the standard use of this logical particle. Accordingly, they would suppose him not to have denied the law of non-contradiction but rather to have employed the symbol "not" in a novel way consistent with that law.[5]

Does this not imply then that the original logical truth "not (p and not-p)" is indeed so self-evidently true that it cannot be denied, and does it not prove that we have here after all a basic truth underlying or capable of underlying all our knowledge? Our interlocutor might insist, however, that in asserting both "p" and "not-p," he claims indeed to be using the classical negation symbol and thus to have succeeded in denying the law of non-contradiction. It might, to the contrary, be argued that his claim is not persuasive; if a statement is true, its denial should at least be coherent if not factual. That is, its non-factuality ought at least to be understandable, though ruled out by its contradictory. In the case of our above logical truth, "not (p and not-p)," by contrast, its formal denial is not even grammatically coherent; it is not ruled out as non-factual by its contradictory, but rather as beyond the boundary of comprehensibility by speakers of the language.

Moreover, this formal denial, since logically false, implies every statement, including the law of non-contradiction itself which it purports to deny. Though possible as a formal statement, this denial is so self-defeating as to keep the object of its denial firmly in place, in consequence erasing the very line between true and false statements and thus eliminating all point to assertion. Implying all assertions, it ends up making none.

Were we, in spite of all this, to concede to the die-hard defender of certainty that the survival of the law of non-contradiction in the face of formal denial is a sign of its certainty rather than an indication of its impotence as a deniable assertion, this concession could hardly be comforting to such defender. For it would be a mere fantasy to imagine that the whole structure of our knowledge could be reared on the foundation of classical logic alone, sole possessor of direct access to truth and sole source of indirect access for every other item of our knowledge.

It is worth noting that Descartes himself, having proved to his own satisfaction that his "Cogito"-statement had achieved certainty, still required a battery of further arguments to support the general trustworthiness of our senses, without thereby denying the occurrence of errors.[6] Such arguments as he provided depended on his proofs of the existence and perfection of God, purporting to show that God could not possibly deceive us, avoidable errors arising nevertheless from unrestrained use of our freedom of will. These supplementary arguments, however, are demonstratively unpersuasive, and clearly incapable of chaining the putative certainty of the "Cogito"-statement to the empirical items to be justified, hence enabling them to achieve indirect access to the truth.

Furthermore, short of the flat denial of classical logic, some theorists, among them assorted intuitionists, constructivists, semanticists, and theoretical physicists, with differing motivations, have in fact proposed the idea of giving up classical logic for various purposes while preserving consistency through adopting one or another deviant logic instead. In this enlarged sense of "denial," classical logic may itself be denied consistently for any of a number of reasons, without, as before, reinstating the very object of its denial. Classical logic can thus hardly be conceived as beyond reasonable revision, hence as certain.[7]

Turning now from rationalistic sources of the emphasis on certainty, we consider empiricistic emphases on sensory experience, purporting to provide us with brute particulars transparently evident to consciousness. The particulars we perceive cannot, it is affirmed, be wished away; they are given to the senses and stand firm amid changing winds of doctrine. They may be interpreted, but they cannot be denied by aspiring theories which are, in fact, tested by them—since they provide hard evidence favoring some and destroying others. Twentieth-century empiricism took its rise in the rejection of philosophical idealism, which gave primacy to the mind and short shrift to sensory particulars in its understanding of knowledge.

6. C. I. Lewis' Empiricism

The American pragmatist C. I. Lewis expressed his criticism of idealism thus: "If the mind were the only condition of the thing as known, then the nature of the mind being specified, objects in general would be completely determined. . . . Unless the content of knowledge is recognized to have a condition independent of the mind, the peculiar significance of knowledge is likely to be lost. For the purpose of knowledge is to be true to something which is beyond it. Its intent is to be governed and dictated to in certain respects. It is a real act with a real purpose because it seeks something which it knows it may miss. If knowledge had no condition independent of the knowing act, would this be so?"[8] This condition Lewis identified as "the sensuously given." We shall focus our ensuing consideration of modern empiricism by attending, in particular, to Lewis' *Mind and the World Order* (1929).

Modern empiricism, in its several various forms, has been inspired by the role of observation and experiment in the natural sciences, where general theories are tested by the independent deliverances of the senses. No theory is certain; rather, it provides a fallible interpretation of the hard data so far given to the senses, ever vulnerable to what further sensory experience may bring, and therefore at best probable. The sensory given is, however, to be thought of quite differently, for Lewis. It is not interpretive nor, therefore, is it fallible. And to require only that theory and conceivable statements of sensory observation be coherent is vacuous as a test of the former. Unless some such statements are independently selected out of their infinitely numerous kin consistent with a proposed theory, we have no basis for assigning the theory any observational merit.

If, for Lewis, the sensory given is to afford us the means of testing a proposed theory, it must be construed as certain, an incorrigible fact of subjective experience, hence capable of restricting the mind's arbitrariness in seeking objective knowledge. Indeed, if it were in its turn also fallible, thus merely probable relative to other premises, and so on, it would provide no basis at all for evaluating the theory in question, either positively or negatively. The chain of probabilities must therefore terminate in certainty, if we can claim to have any empirical knowledge at all.

This brief for certainty has been disputed by Nelson Goodman, who begins by agreeing with Lewis that "credibility may be transmitted from one statement to another through deductive or probability connections; but credibility does not spring from these connections by spontaneous generation. Somewhere along the line some statements . . . must have initial credibility."[9] But here Goodman adds the words, ". . . credibility to some degree, not certainty." In arguing against mere coherence as a way of anchoring the chain of probabilities with which we started, Goodman is thus at one with Lewis. But he thinks the appeal to certainty is excessive, since initial credibility alone provides the required anchorage, without blocking the possibility of overturning such credibility in the future. Thus, no statement whatever is immune to withdrawal, yet the initial credibility of statements at a time exercises a degree of control over the system of statements as a whole that cannot be blithely ignored or dealt with arbitrarily.

I have found Goodman's argument persuasive, and have interpreted initial credibilities as reflecting "our varied inclinations to affirm given statements as true or assert them as scientifically acceptable: equivalently, they may be construed as indicating the initial claims we recognize statements to make upon us, at any given time, for inclusion within our cognitive systems."[10] Russell's superficially similar notion of "intrinsic credibility" is actually quite different from "initial credibility" in importing the unwanted suggestion of credibility values as fixed over time, whereas it seems evident that our inclinations to affirm particular statements vary considerably from time to time and imply no immunity to revision.[11]

There are additional problems with Lewis' conception of the given. His main concern, as Goodman acknowledges, is not to find sentences that are certain, hence suitable to serve as axioms of a system of knowledge; rather it is to recognize that empirical knowledge rests on error-free sensory contents subject to fallible conceptual interpretation. It is, however, difficult to see how an error-free given at a particular moment can serve as a check on theory. For once the momentary given is gone, the memory of its past character provides no error-free testimony for or against the theory in question, only a fallible interpretation of what the present memory signifies about the past moment.

Further, Lewis admits that the given is intertwined with interpretation. "The independence of the given," he holds, "[does not] entail the practical possibility of removing altogether the encrustation of concepts, so as to discover the core of the given in a moment of sheer apprehension."[12] How, then, one might ask, is the given itself to serve as a check on theory?

If Lewis' aim is simply to show that the given, though never unqualified by thought and always "an excised element or abstraction," is at least not "an 'unreal' abstraction" but "an identifiable constituent in experience," he needs to tell us how to identify it analytically. This, he declares, we can do by focusing on the sensuous aspect of experience, and then by attending to the quality of unalterability by thought, the given being "unaffected by any change of mental attitude or interest." The given, in sum, is "that which remains untouched and unaltered, however it is construed by thought."[13]

That anything is thus untouched seems to me at variance with the psychological facts as represented by both anecdotal reports and experimental evidence. Both such sources affirm the enormous influence exercised by belief, expectation, and set in determining the quality of the sensuous given. Ample anecdotal support for such influence is supplied by numerous sources, of which Ernst Gombrich's *Art and Illusion* will serve as a representative sample of illustrations drawn from certain technical areas, from the history of art, and from everyday life. The tendency of such illustrations is to counterpose the maxim "Seeing is believing" with its often more germane obverse, "Believing is seeing." In this connection, Gombrich tells us that "Intelligence officers intent on the reading of aerial reconnaissance photographs, X-ray specialists basing a diagnosis on the faintest of shadows visible in a tissue, learn in a hard school how often 'believing is seeing' and how important it therefore is to keep their hypothesis flexible."[14]

One empirical psychological study will here serve for many: D. C. McClelland and J. W. Atkinson measured the effect of hunger upon the images projected by subjects onto a blank screen. "After a preliminary phase in which faint images were actually shown on the screen, the experimenters exposed blanks but asked for description of the things shown; they found that food-related responses, and even the size of imagined food objects, increased with the increase of hunger."[15] Cases familiar in ordinary experience are instanced by M. Sherif and H. Cantril, who cite "the case of the hungry man looking for bread or the case of a lover waiting in a crowd for his sweetheart."[16]

The main problem with Lewis' conception, however, is that the notion of an error-free or certain given is confused. "Error and certainty, like truth and falsehood, are purported characteristics of descriptions, not in general of things described."[17] The sense in which the sensory given is not subject to error simply reflects the fact that it is no description; this fact by no means implies that reports of the given are immune from mistake. The error-free character of the given is thus a triviality, of no epistemological interest whatever. I conclude, in sum, that empiricist views may be no more anchored in the safety of certainty than are rationalist ones.

Having rejected the various appeals to certainty as terminating the justification chains purporting to give our beliefs their indirect access to truth, we shall do well to revisit three controlling ideas that have given rise to the original problem of relating justification to truth. One such idea is that of access to truth, a second is that of justification itself, and the third is that of certainty.

7. Access as a Metaphor

Access to truth is a metaphor, natural enough and seemingly harmless. But it brings with it consequences equally natural though not at all harmless. The expression "access to truth" invites us to see attainment of access as a process analogous to physical access to a room, a transition from outside a closed space to its inside. No belief, it has been widely asserted, has direct access to truth; every belief either lacks access altogether or, at best, has indirect access, achieved only through justification by evidence. Indeed, that no belief has direct access is what is said to necessitate recourse to justification, constituting the only means of transition from outside all access to attainable, that is to say, indirect access. Acquiring justification is, on this view, a historical process, since no belief is born with its justification on its face, at best gaining indirect access by acquiring suitable evidential relations to other beliefs.

Assume, then, a given belief with no such apparent relations upon its initial formulation. Having later been shown to acquire such relations to evidential premises, has it thereby been justified and gained indirect access to truth? Clearly, if these premises are unjustified, themselves lacking access, their consequences also lack access, hence providing no justification for the belief in question, and moving it not a whit closer to the truth sought. And if, as some have suggested, the premises in question are in their turn shown to be appropriately linked to still others, the question recurs as to whether these presumably evidential others are themselves justified. No matter how long the purported justification chain is imagined to extend, unless it is somehow anchored to truth, it is idling, running in place, no closer to achieving access for our initial belief than it had to begin with.

The classical solution to this problem has been to reject the critical assumption that no belief has direct access to the truth. Once we affirm, with many thinkers, both rationalists and empiricists, that some beliefs are in fact certain, possessed of direct access to truth, other beliefs can theoretically, through suitable logical or probabilistic linkages to these, acquire indirect access to truth, thus attaining justification without fear of endless regress. This strategy, as we have noted, requires designation of those beliefs thought to be certain and, moreover, rich enough to generate all the desired justified content, and we have already seen the difficulties this involves. Without this strategy, however, how can we interpret justification, required by all accounts to make sense of the knowledge we claim, and, moreover, without reliance on the discredited notion of certainty?

8. J. F. Fries and K. Popper

A general proposal for achieving this goal is to replace recourse to certainty with the adoption of a convention for the making of a decision: we simply decree that certain beliefs are to be taken, for the moment, as having direct access to the truth and we justify other beliefs by linking them to these. A more specific and elaborate formulation of such a proposal is that of Popper, following J. F. Fries, who argued that "if the statements of science are not to be accepted dogmatically, we must be able to justify them."[18] To insist, however, that all statements are to be logically justified, warns Fries, leads to an infinite regress. "Now, if we wish to avoid the danger of dogmatism as well as an infinite regress, then it seems as if we could only have recourse to psychologism, i.e. the doctrine that statements can be justified not only by statements but also by perceptual experience."[19] Fries chose psychologism, the appeal to sense experience as yielding immediate knowledge. Popper himself, however, rejects psychologism since, he argues, no statement of sense experience is immune from testing and possible revision. He further holds that in testing a theory by reference to basic statements, there is no absolute stopping point, since every such statement is open to further tests; every test of a theory in fact "must stop at some basic statement or other which we decide to accept."[20]

Popper's resolution of Fries' trilemma is to replace recourse to certainty, while avoiding psychologism, with the adoption of a convention or the making of a decision: We simply decree that certain beliefs are to be taken, for the moment, as tantamount to having direct access to the truth, and we justify other beliefs by linking them to these. Such decrees obviously lack certainty since we are free to renounce them at will by issuing new decrees. They are, in this sense, impermanent but, so long as they are in force, they may be assumed to justify any claims for which they provide evidential support. As he elaborates, "The basic statements at which we stop, which we decide to accept as satisfactory, and as sufficiently tested, have admittedly the character of dogmas. . . . But this kind of dogmatism is innocuous since, should the need arise, these statements can easily be tested further."

9. Voluntarism and Linearity

Two problems confront the recourse to *convention, decision, or decree* in the interpretation of justification. One problem is that of *voluntarism*; the other is that of *linearity*. The reliance on decree (which here stands in for any of the three notions) is what I refer to as voluntarism, since it poses no constraint on the adoption of any decree at any time. Such voluntarism does, as intended, free the strategy from appeal to certainty—only, however, to saddle it with the stigma of dogmatism, since no decree itself requires to be justified. It is serial dogmatism to be sure, but dogmatism nonetheless, having, as Bertrand Russell once said of the method of postulation, all the advantages of theft over honest toil. As long, further, as we are willing to condone such thievery, what precludes us from using it directly for all the several beliefs we hope to justify as gaining indirect access, or as having passed a relevant test, rather than restricting it to the premises from which we hope to derive such beliefs?

What I refer to as linearity is the property, shared by the classical and the present (decisional) conception, of a chain, which starts with a fixed point or points neither requiring nor, indeed, allowing any justification, and proceeds by logical or probabilistic derivation to further steps which are justified thereby. Whether the initial starting points are thought to be either certainties or free decrees does not affect the property of linearity common to both conceptions.

This property has the effect of treating every one of our beliefs as guilty unless proven innocent, that is, as unjustified (or as not serviceable) unless shown to be suitably linked to starting points that are certain (for the classical conception) or decreed (for the decisional conception). The former makes the barrier to justification impossibly high since, as we have seen, certainty is beyond our reach, and hence treating all our beliefs as unjustified. The latter virtually abolishes the barrier altogether, counting all beliefs as justifiable (or serviceable) at will. Both uphold the view that if our beliefs are to pass muster, they can do so only by having recourse either to mythical certainties (in the one case) or willful decisions (in the other).

10. One-Way Justification

A corollary of the view held in common by both conceptions is that the first link in a given justification chain must be assumed firm since its role is to anchor the chain. The first link justifies; it cannot itself waver or be overridden by subsequent links. The justification process is one-way only. This picture, as we have seen earlier, is similar to that of Lewis, who regards the given as incorrigible, and contrasts with Goodman's notion of statements with initial credibility, always vulnerable to overthrow by other such statements with higher credibility. We shall have occasion later to compare these two conceptions as intended accounts of justification in the sciences, but for now let us ask what the consequences would be if both voluntarism and linearity were surrendered.

In a word, the effect would be far-reaching. The notion of starting from scratch would be given up, and justification would no longer be conceived as chainlike, patterned after a logical or mathematical proof. Our beliefs would no longer carry the burden of original guilt unless and until proven innocent. Justification as a deliberate procedure would not be thought of as an initial qualifying process, required for admission into our body of beliefs, but rather as a subsequent process, taking place after the fact, and only as needed. Starting with our initial mass of beliefs as given, we would in effect treat them as innocent until proven guilty, reversing the onus of justification. Justifiable control over our body of beliefs would not be centered in one source, but diffused through the mass, exercising democratic rather than autocratic authority. Such a large overhauling of the classical and the decisional conceptions has already in fact been accomplished through the pioneering work of philosophical pragmatists and pragmatically inclined thinkers inspired by the empirical sciences.

11. Beginning in the Middle

We have earlier made reference to Peirce's insistence that we begin always in the middle of things, our minds already stocked with beliefs which, we may note, he considered to function in the manner of habits. That is, they are to be considered as approximating dispositions, readinesses, sets to act in response to contingencies that might arise in the future. These are to be thought of as positive or negative in valence, either attractive or repulsive, tropisms or aversions, but in any event providing a structure of potential actions with which we face the future. The question of their several justifications *de novo* is manifestly absurd. The very notion of justification is a sophisticated achievement not available prior to the availability of beliefs. Nor could justification, however understood, proceed without taking certain beliefs for granted, prior to their own justification. Wholesale initial justification is a fantasy.

Peirce's essay, "The Fixation of Belief"[21] presents a statement of his theory of inquiry. Doubt differs from belief in three respects: (a) "There is

a dissimilarity between the sensation of doubting and that of believing."
(b) "The feeling of believing is a more or less sure indication of there being
established in our nature some habit which will determine our actions.
Doubt never has such an effect." (c) "Doubt is an uneasy and dissatisfied
state from which we struggle to free ourselves and pass into the state of
belief, while the latter is a calm and satisfactory state which we do not wish
to avoid, or to change to a belief in anything else. On the contrary, we cling
tenaciously, not merely to believing, but to believing just what we do
believe."

The function of beliefs so understood by Peirce and elaborated correspondingly by William James and John Dewey in particular, is to constitute
a stable platform for response, should the need arise. Thought itself is
activated when problems intrude themselves upon us, our cluster of dispositions to respond incapable of overt realization either because of internal short-circuiting or owing to external impediments. Thought is then
specific, directed toward the initiating problem of recovering overt realization of our stalled dispositional cluster, to the end of attaining stability of
habits again.

12. Justification, Contextual and Comparative

Peirce was influenced by his conception of laboratory science, focusing
always on particular questions arising in the context of prior science, and
taking its inherited conclusions provisionally for granted. Scientific investigations, following this model, do not seek to investigate nor, certainly, to
justify the inherited totality of scientific beliefs. Directing their attention to
the particular locus of an initiating problem, such investigations strive
to bring the relevant embedded assumptions to light, scrutinizing
possible alterations, deletions, or additions that show promise of
resolving the problem in question. Deciding, in favorable cases, on a projected solution, they need then to justify such a course as against its alternatives. Justification here comes into play for the first time in its natural
habitat. Beliefs not surviving the competition with alternatives are then
treated as not justified for the present while the winners are accorded
justification.

Thus conceived, justification does not provide access to a magic circle
of truths protected by a single entry gate. Rather, it provides a provisional

improvement in our cluster of beliefs, freeing it from the recent problem we have striven to overcome. We affirm this cluster now, reserving our right to alter it for cause later on. Similarly, we remain open to the possibility of further problems that may arise tomorrow, but sufficient unto the day is the problem thereof. Once having recovered the stability of our relevant cluster of assumptions, we can continue to use it in assertion, application, invention, and exploration until presently unforeseen difficulties arise, requiring future treatments similar to those hitherto provided but impossible to imagine in advance.

Justification thus conceived is not an eternal state—once justified, always justified. It is relative to context at a time, thus alterable for locally pertinent reasons. It is, further, ordinarily comparative, the justified solution having won out over alternative candidates for an optimum solution to a problem. Without specification of the problem, neither justification nor its lack has any clear sense. Unlike the effect of the linearity property, there is here no presumption that every one of our beliefs is guilty unless proven innocent. To affirm that a belief is abstractly justified or not is like affirming that Iowa is east, without answering the obvious query: "East of what?" A reversal of a fundamental sort has thus taken place with surrender of linearity.

I have earlier criticized linearity mainly by noting its requirement for chainlike justifications to be anchored by unacceptable starting points, whether certainties or decrees. A decisive difficulty with linearity is its radical mismatch with processes of justification in empirical science, as distinct from mathematical proof. Enunciated forcefully by Peirce, his argument is that a mathematical proof, understood as proceeding by logical steps from unquestioned premises to unquestioned conclusions, is, like any chain, no stronger than its weakest link, and incapable of transmitting more strength to its conclusions than is evident in its premises. Both these features are manifestly absent among characteristically recurrent forms of justification salient in the empirical sciences.[22]

13. Justification in the Empirical Sciences

Theoretical premises in these sciences are not offered as certainties transmitting certainty to their derivations, which clearly contain no more strength than they themselves contain. Formulated as axioms though they may be, they are nevertheless offered not as unquestioned truths but rather as conjectural hypotheses. In a process Peirce labels "abductive," such hypotheses gain their support through systematizing a variety of initially credible beliefs which, as a result, turn out surprisingly related and, moreover, explainable, assuming the conjectural theory true.[23] Support in such cases flows upward to the conjectured theory from the relevant empirical beliefs rather than downward from theoretical premises certain in themselves. Thereafter, the theory combines with other credible beliefs, the combination yielding empirical consequences either deductively or probabilistically, thus now contributing to the downward flow of support.

A successful theory thus construed turns out to be vastly stronger than any particular empirical belief that has contributed its share to the upward flow, and may in fact survive the later falsification of any such belief, or beliefs, if enough others continue to hold. Unlike the chain which is no stronger than its weakest link, the pattern of support here wants a different metaphor, which Peirce indeed supplies in the image of a cable which, strong as it is, is composed of a variety of interwoven slender strands, each weaker and shorter than the cable itself, each moreover dispensable, provided enough others remain intact for the nonce. Reasoning in empirical science, Peirce insists, is "circumstantial, multiform, hypothetical, explanatory. Building only on modestly firm data, the web it forms is extremely powerful."[24]

Examples of outstanding scientific theories fitting the description just provided abound. The theory of evolution, for example, rests not on indubitable premises initiating a logical chain, or chains, ending in this theory as its conclusion. Rather, it gains support as it organizes and systematizes a number of results drawn from disparate empirical sciences, including paleontology, comparative anatomy and physiology, blood chemistry, stratigraphy, genetics, etc.—results which, seemingly scattered, turn out unexpectedly related and, indeed, partially explainable in evolutionary terms. The general theory itself has in this process gained more strength than any of the particular beliefs on which it rests, and may survive any number of these provided enough others remain after they are gone. However, no matter how strong it may eventually become, it never achieves certainty, nor does it in itself by deduction alone generate empirical results.

We have now apparently dispensed with the troubles of linearity in interpreting justification. But a new problem begins to loom: the threat of circularity. For consider: The theory which rests on, i.e., is justified by, particular empirical beliefs in turn explains, hence justifies them. The theory is, in other words, justified by the very beliefs which it eventually helps to justify, and the beliefs in question are justified by the very theory ultimately resting on themselves. Does this not give the impossible upshot that the theory justifies itself and that each belief justifies itself as well? Surely, with support flowing both upward and downward, there must be a short circuit in this line of reasoning. The way back to linearity is blocked and the way forward to circularity seems to guarantee obvious failure. What to do?

14. Circularity versus Linearity

A critical feature of the problem requires notice: the fact that each of its elements has a double, not a single, potential source of support. Every empirical belief in the sciences and every conjectural theory therein has its own (possibly zero) degree of credibility *before* the question of justification arises. The combined empirical results justified by a theory do not for that reason alone qualify as supporting the very theory in question. To qualify in this respect, they must in addition be judged as sufficiently credible on their own merits.

Nor does the theoretical conjecture itself rest exclusively on the empirical results which support it. It has, in addition, some degree of credibility of its own, as a result of its fit with other credible theories, and the limited support already garnered by its capacity to explain and to predict empirical beliefs other than the ones under present consideration.

15. Democratic Controls

Justification is in effect not limited to a tight circle in which nothing extraneous intrudes. Each of the two main elements, i.e., theory and belief, is simultaneously sensitive to the other while retaining a measure of its own independence. No element is immune to change, free of all control by the other, but neither is such control absolute. Control, as we have already noted, is not autocratic but democratic, diffused throughout the whole realm of beliefs, in which each is both subject and object of control.

A familiar example of this form of wide circularity, which is not only not fallacious but also obviously useful, is the ordinary dictionary, in which a given word may be defined in terms of another, and that one in turn by another, and so forth, until, after a while, the last member of the series may return to the first. As in the case that has just concerned us, each ordinary word involved here has two potential sources of clarification, its own independent, but implicit and uncodified, usage and the dictionary definition, which offers a formula explicitly relating it to other words. Usage may override a dictionary definition, but a definition may revise usage. The control that each exercises over the other is certainly not absolute but neither is it altogether powerless. In the interaction between them lies the utility of dictionaries.

Some writers have distinguished the case of science from the typical example of a fallacious circle consisting of a small number of elements, by arguing that the width of the scientific circle sets it apart. In this vein, Morris R. Cohen and Ernest Nagel affirm the general account given above, as follows:

> There is a sense in which all science is circular, for all proof rests upon assumptions which are not derived from others but are justified by the set of consequences which are deduced from them. Thus we correct our observations and free them of errors by appeal to principles, and yet these principles are justified only because they are in agreement with the readings which result from experiment. In other words, science cannot rest on principles alone. Nor can it rest on experimental observations regarded as all free and equal. Each is used to check the other. But there is a difference between a circle consisting of a small number of propositions, from which we can escape by denying them all or setting up their contradictories, and the circle of theoretical science and human observation, which is so wide that we cannot set up any alternative to it.[25]

The difference between width and narrowness here pointed out is certainly apt and it is perhaps generally true that the narrower a circle the more likely its viciousness. But this is not always the case, the critical feature being rather the fact that the elements of virtuous circles have two sources of support, not one. Thus, while the circular dictionary definition, as typically illustrated, travels a wide path before returning to its origin, even a definition with only two elements may not be vicious in that each has an independent background of usage with which it enters the dictionary equation connecting them. This usage exercises partial control over future use, as does the equation itself. Usage and equation interact, each in principle capable of modifying the other.

16. Interactionism

The interactional view of justification, an offshoot of Peirce's anti-Cartesian view of science, is seen as well in Goodman's justification of induction as a matter of "making mutual adjustments between rules and accepted inferences;—in the agreement achieved lies the only justification needed for either." It figures, too, in law as exhibited in the continuous interplay between precedent and statute; in ethics as exemplified by Rawls' phrase "reflective equilibrium," as well as my "On Justification and Commitment" (see Chapter 5); in Quine's pragmatism; and in White's holism, as embracing both science and morals.[26]

Notes

1   Laurence Bonjour, *The Structure of Empirical Knowledge* (Cambridge, MA: Harvard University Press, 1985), pp. 7–8. Quoted, with additional examples of the main point by other authors, in Harvey Siegel, "Truth, Thinking, Testimony and Trust: Alvin Goldman on Epistemology and Education," *Philosophy and Phenomenological Research* 71, no. 2 (2005): 351–53.

2   René Descartes, *Discourse on Method*, Part Four, and *Meditations on First Philosophy*, First and Second Meditations.

3   Cf. A. J. Ayer, *The Problem of Knowledge* (Harmondsworth, Middlesex: Penguin Books, 1956), pp. 44–57, and my *Conditions of Knowledge* (Chicago: Scott Foresman, 1965), ch. 3.

4   See A. N. Whitehead and B. Russell, *Principia Mathematica*, 3 vols. (Cambridge, UK: Cambridge University Press, 1910, 1912, 1913), and W. V. Quine, *Set Theory and Its Logic* (Cambridge, MA: Belknap Press of Harvard University Press, 1969).

5   See W. V. Quine, *Philosophy of Logic* (Englewood Cliffs, NJ: Prentice-Hall, 1970), ch. 6.

6   Descartes, *Meditations*, op. cit., Fourth Meditation.

7   Quine, *Philosophy of Logic*, op. cit., and see Susan Haack, *Deviant Logic* (Cambridge, UK: Cambridge University Press, 1974), and Haack, *Deviant Logic, Fuzzy Logic* (Chicago: University of Chicago Press, 1996).

8   Clarence Irving Lewis, *Mind and the World Order* (New York: Dover, 1956), pp. 189–92.

9   See Nelson Goodman, "Sense and Certainty," *Philosophical Review* 61 (1952): 160–67, and C. I. Lewis, "The Given Element in Empirical Knowledge," *Philosophical Review* 61 (1952): 168–75.

10 Israel Scheffler, *Science and Subjectivity*, 2nd ed. (Indianapolis: Hackett, 1985), pp. 116, 123.

11 Bertrand Russell, *Human Knowledge, Its Scope and Limits* (New York: Simon and Schuster, 1948), part 2, ch.11; part 5, chs. 5–7.

12 See Lewis, op. cit., p. 66, and Scheffler, op. cit., p. 26.

13 Lewis, op. cit.

14 E. H. Gombrich, *Art and Illusion* (Washington: Pantheon, 1956), pp. 88, 204.

15 D. C. McClelland and J. W. Atkinson, "The Projective Expression of Needs: I. The Effect of Different Intensities of the Hunger Drive on Perception," *Journal of Psychology* 25 (1948): 205–22.

16 Muzafer Sherif and Hadley Cantril, *The Psychology of Ego-Involvements* (New York: John Wiley & Sons, 1947), p. 32, and Scheffler, *Science and Subjectivity*, op. cit., pp. 30–31.

17 Scheffler, ibid., 34.

18 J. F. Fries, *Neue oder anthropologische Kritik der Vernunft* (1828 to 1831), discussed extensively by K. R. Popper, *The Logic of Scientific Discovery* (London: Hutchinson, 1959), ch. 5, pp. 93–111. The quotations in this paragraph represent Popper's understanding of the view of Fries, who opted for psychologism.

19 Popper, ibid., p. 104.

20 Ibid., pp. 104–5.

21 C. S. Peirce, *Collected Papers of Charles Sanders Peirce*, Charles Hartshorne and Paul Weiss, eds., vols. 1–6 (Cambridge, MA: Harvard University Press, 1931–35), 5.372, and Scheffler, *Four Pragmatists*, op. cit., p. 60.

22 C.S.P., *Collected Papers*, 5.265, and Scheffler, *Four Pragmatists*, op. cit., p. 52.

23 C.S.P., *Collected Papers*, 3.516, and 5.171 on abduction.

24 Scheffler, *Four Pragmatists*, op. cit., p. 54.

25 Morris R. Cohen and Ernest Nagel, *An Introduction to Logic and Scientific Method* (New York: Harcourt Brace, 1934), p. 379.

26 Nelson Goodman, *Fact, Fiction and Forecast*, 4th ed. (Cambridge, MA: Harvard University Press, 1983), p. 64; see also John Rawls, *A Theory of Justice* (Cambridge, MA; Harvard University Press, 1971), pp. 48–51. Israel Scheffler,

"On Justification and Commitment," *Journal of Philosophy* 51 (1954): 180–90, reprinted here as Chapter 5. W. V. Quine, *From a Logical Point of View*, 2d ed. (Cambridge, MA: Harvard University Press, 1961), ch. 2, and Morton White, *A Philosophy of Culture* (Princeton, NJ: Princeton University Press, 2002).

Chapter 2

Truth

These latter remarks illustrate the fact that the interactional view, as well as the notion of justification itself pertains not only to assertions in science, but also to rules, norms, laws, and acts. We here shall take sentences, as expressive of statements or assertions (inclusive of, but not limited to, empirical theories), as our primary objects of present interest, and adopt the interactional view of justification as our working assumption. The question we now confront is this: What is the relation of justification to truth or, more specifically, how does the predicate "is justified," applicable to sentences, relate to the predicate "is true"?

Having earlier rid ourselves of certainty, that is, of direct access to truth, and resigned ourselves to indirect access at best through *linear* justification or to sentences justified by *interactional* justification, is it indeed truth to which justification gives us access? Does it, in other words, authorize us to call a justified sentence "true," as direct access does for sentences deemed certain? To this question, many thinkers have been increasingly inclined to answer with a resounding "No," balking at overreaching beyond what they think they have a right to claim. The ironic net result of a sentence's attaining the status of having been justified, with its implied right to be asserted as true, is the retirement of the predicate "is true" from active epistemological service altogether, in favor of direct access rather to "is justified," or analogous terms such as "is confirmed," "is verified," or the ever more popular "is probable."

The word "true" may of course be retained by those who refuse to call any sentence flatly true, provided they relativize its use and interpret it as equivalent to the relative notions of confirmation, verification, etc., which vary with time, person, and circumstance. The traditional, classical notion of truth is, by contrast, absolute or categorical, every closed sentence within a given language considered true or false, without relativization to such variable factors as those mentioned previously.

To be sure, if we focus simply on the physical marks or sounds underlying a given sentence in a certain language, we must acknowledge that they may underlie quite a different sentence in another language, thus implying relativity once more. Such relativity pertains, however, not to full-bodied, interpreted sentences but only to their physical substrates, thus differing from the recent epistemological relativity noted previously as at odds with classical notions.[1]

Prior to turning to the challenge of this recent relativity to the notion of absolute truth, we may note, in passing, the quite different, ancient challenge presented by the paradox of the Liar—a sentence affirming its own denial, e.g., "I am lying," "this sentence is false." A recent explicit and clearer formulation by Quine is this: "'Yields a falsehood when appended to its own quotation' yields a falsehood when appended to its own quotation." This and related paradoxes can be overcome if truth locutions are, actually or tacitly, ordered hierarchically by numerical subscripts, and then making sure that any such locution is applied to a sentence only when its subscript is higher than any within the sentence in question. With such safeguards against the Liar in place (and barring future threats from as yet unencountered paradoxes), epistemological relativity assumes prominence once more as a prevalent challenge to absolute truth.[2]

1. Allergy to Absolute Truth

The widespread allergy to absolute or categorical truth and its replacement by one or another relative notion faces an insuperable problem, however, in the specter of an infinite regress. For suppose a given sentence S to be justified. The sentence S1 (i.e., "S is justified") cannot, of course, itself be declared by the relativizers to be categorically true. The best they can do is to affirm S2 (i.e., "'S is justified' is justified"). And, to the further question whether or not S2 in its turn is justified, to reply by affirming S3, and so on, without end. Relativization has thus given us only two options for assessing S: either to deny that it is justified or to affirm it to be justified, without, however, being able flatly to justify this affirmation itself. Like "is true," "is justified" has thus also been removed from epistemological service, in consequence depriving us of two major instruments for assessing the worth of our beliefs.

What factors have gotten us into this sorry predicament? I think we can single out three main culprits. One is the prevalent metaphor of access to truth, which we have already had occasion to criticize. Another is the misunderstanding of certainty as a corollary of truth. The third is a confusion of the import of truth with methods of estimating it, or deciding what to take as true.

Let us begin first with a brief remark on access to truth in relation to the empirical sciences. Since a major source of the critique of absolute truth is the influence of these sciences and their rejection of certainty, we find it natural to imagine a radical incongruity between science and truth, with science yielding a parade of theories, each justified only for the moment and replaceable by its successor, while truth is conceived as an exclusive realm yielding direct access only to permanent certainties and indirect access perhaps not at all, as we have seen. With these alternatives to choose from, there is clearly no contest, the resulting imperative being the relativization of truth, and its disastrous infinite regress, noted previously.

2. Provisionality and Truth

If the absolute predicate "is true," no matter how interpreted, is taken to imply "is certain," there is independent reason to eschew it, even were we to give up the metaphor of access to truth. It has therefore seemed obvious to many thinkers, philosophers as well as scientists, that having given up certainty, in accord with the anti-dogmatic spirit of science, we need to surrender absolute truth as well. William James, in this vein, champions the relativization of truth as "simply a collective name for verification processes . . . Truth is *made*, just as health, wealth and strength are made, in the course of experience."[3] James goes on to attribute to defenders of the classical notion of truth (whom he refers to as intellectualists) the assumption that "truth means essentially an inert static relation. When you've got your true idea of anything, there's an end of the matter. You're in possession; you know; you have fulfilled your thinking destiny."

The implicit view here expressed is that to affirm a sentence as true is to bind oneself forever after to this affirmation—"there's an end of the matter."[4] Overlooked is the familiar possibility that, having judged a given sentence as true, one is free to change one's mind and to alter this judgment later, when new evidence appears. The provisional character of our several truth judgments is perfectly compatible with understanding truth as absolute rather than relative. It is one thing to impute absolute truth to a sentence at a given time, thus claiming it at that time to possess an invariable property; it is quite another to suppose that this claim is itself invariable, binding us for eternity and barring us from ever altering our judgment.

In sum, the import of a truth claim is the attribution, at a given time, of a categorical property or relation, of any degree; no further claim of certainty for this attribution itself is implied. The attribution itself, as distinguished from the property or relation attributed, is provisional, and such provisionality suffices to block certainty. A sentence we estimate at a given time as true, taking it at that time to be true, may thus be taken later as untrue. But "true" and "taken to be true" are quite different predicates, the former being absolute, the latter relative to time and person. A sentence S, if true, is simply true, without qualification, though it is false that S, taken to be true here and now by me, is always and everywhere taken to be true by everyone. The variability of our takings-to-be true is to be sharply distinguished from truth itself.

A laudable motive for relativizing truth is to avoid dogmatism, in sympathy with the spirit and practice of science. Science indeed opposes dogmatism, but dogmatism rests on a conviction of certainty, not absolute truth. If relativizers such as James and many others are interpreted as essentially concerned with opposing certainty, they are then on firm ground, though mistaken in framing their opposition as an attack on absolute truth.

We have named three culprits in moving us to relativize truth, while making it virtually impossible even to apply the relative notion. Of these three, we have so far criticized two: the metaphor of access to truth and the idea that truth implies certainty. We have yet to consider the third, consisting in a confusion of the import of truth with methods for deciding which sentences to take as true. Such methods are notably multifarious, varying with the content of the sentences to be assessed for truth. To decide the truth candidacy of sentences in astronomy, for example, we employ methods quite different from those employed in the fields of history, or zoology, or psychiatry, or linguistics, or literary criticism, each field of inquiry requiring its own characteristic means for estimating the truth of sentences within its realm. The methods are relevantly diverse, but it clearly does not follow that the import of truth attribution varies from field to field and even from one specialization within a given field to another. The argument that truth must be interpreted as relative since the methods of its estimation vary from area to area is therefore wholly without merit.

3. Truth versus Verification

Having defended the classical notion of truth by criticizing three outstanding sources of its rejection by relativizers, we now consider several independent arguments against the reduction of truth to verification or confirmation, or justification, or the like.[5] We typically suppose a sentence to be either true or false in accord with the principle of excluded middle. But some sentences, although they are true or false, have not been verified by us to be true nor to be false. We cannot now, for instance, confirm that Caesar had breakfast the day he crossed the Rubicon nor can we confirm that he did not. Yet we must acknowledge that he either did or did not and, accordingly, that it is either true that he did or true that he did not, even though we do not know which it is. According to the principle of excluded middle, if the sentence S is not true then the sentence Not-S is true. But if "true" is interpreted as "confirmed," the principle fails, since if Caesar's having had breakfast on the fateful day (B) is not confirmed (parallel to saying B is not true), it does not follow that Not-B is indeed confirmed (parallel to saying Not-B is indeed true). Neither B nor Not-B is now confirmed (by us) but either B or Not-B is true, though we know not which.

We typically assume also the law of non-contradiction, that no sentence is both true and false. Yet some sentences are confirmed for some persons at a given time but not for others at the same or any other time. If I am sufficiently skilled at hiding the pain of my toothache from my family, they will have good reason to deny that I indeed have a toothache, while I will have adequate and painful reason for affirming that I do. Yet it is not both true and false that I have a toothache, despite its being both confirmed and not confirmed that I do.

Consider now changes in the confirmation status of a scientific theory over time. If a given theory has proved itself predictively adequate and has satisfied every other accepted scientific criterion throughout a given period and then has been decisively disconfirmed, we do not describe it as having first been true and as having later become false. We say rather that it had been for a time taken as (or considered to be) true and then judged to be false. Otherwise, we should be driven to suppose that the physical phenomena themselves change along with our changing physical theories: So long as Newtonian theory was taken to be true, it *was* true—that is, nature *was* Newtonian. With the breakdown of Newtonianism, nature ceased its Newtonian ways and became Einsteinian. To be sure, nature does change, but what reason is there to suppose that it changes obediently every time an accepted fundamental theory is disconfirmed and replaced by a successor?

Further, since each such theory purports to describe not merely large regions of nature but what is always and everywhere the case, the envisaged change is ruled out. It is logically absurd to hold that first one theory and then a quite incompatible one was true—as distinct from holding that first the one and then the conflicting one was *taken* to be true. It is the conflict between these theories that indeed forces a choice beween them since the law of non-contradiction bars their both being true. It rules out their compatibility unless they are newly restricted in scope so that Newtonianism, rather than a universal theory, is now to be understood as applying only for a limited period of time, ending with the advent of Einsteinianism, understood now as starting afresh at the same time. Were these ostensible theories thus reinterpreted as compatible, there would be no logical pressure to choose between them and no scientific motive for the theoretical progress that was actually spurred by their original incompatibility.

Historical examples are even more striking: It used to be thought that Galileo dropped iron balls from the leaning tower of Pisa. It is now generally held that this story is a myth, no longer thought, as before, to be true. Now we cannot suppose that it was for a time true that Galileo did at some time drop iron balls from the tower and that thereafter it became true that he never did. Either he did at some time or he never did; the truth in this matter is not mutable, although of course our estimates or opinions as to what the truth is are surely subject to change.[6]

It is instructive to note that James himself, in defending the mutability of truth, seems inconsistent on the critical issue we have been discussing. He says, on the one hand, that earlier theories *were* true within their "borders of experience" and that earlier processes were "truth-processes for the actors in them though not for us." Yet, on the other hand, he also says that our retrospective judgments *were true* despite earlier thinkers, shedding a "backward light" on the past. He even admits that the views of earlier thinkers are false "absolutely" (putting quotation marks around the word), since the borders of their experience *might* conceivably have been transcended. Indeed, all he seems to have succeeded in showing is that what is taken to be true changes from time to time with the progress of inquiry, but he seems to ackowledge that whatever is taken, at a particular time, to be true is taken to be true absolutely, for there are (as we have seen) logical difficulties in *taking* the same idea to be now true, now false. In sum, variability characterizes estimation of the truth, not truth itself.[7]

4. Truth and Fixity

Some have equated the absoluteness of truth with the fixity of obviously variable natural processes, thus easily refuting the former. But the equation is fallacious, for the two ideas are quite independent. Truth is an attribute of sentences, statements, beliefs, propositions, or ideas, not an attribute of natural things, processes, or events generally. To say that truth is absolute is to say that whatever true sentences affirm is unqualifiedly the case; no further requirement stipulates that true sentences must affirm only constancies or fixities. Whatever changes are to be described, their purported descriptions, if true, are true absolutely. Fluid historical processes or transient historical events do not require fluidity or transiency in the truth of their true descriptions. We have already noted the absurdity of supposing it to be initially true and thereafter false that Galileo at some time in his life dropped iron balls from the leaning tower of Pisa; either it is true absolutely that at some time in his life he did, or it is true absolutely that he never at any time did so.

Similarly, the absolute truth of the statement that the First World War began in 1914 does not imply the absurdity that the war's beginning is timeless, that the war is, for all time, in a state of incipiency. Spatial as well as temporal qualifications of all sorts apply to things describable by true statements, but this does not imply that the truth itself is similarly qualified. If it rained in Boston on June 20, 2005, the sentence "It rained in Boston on June 20, 2005" is not true just in Boston nor is it true just on June 20, 2005; it is simply true.

Insofar, then, as a relativistic doctrine of truth is motivated by the need to take account of the fluidity of history and the pervasiveness of natural change, the same purpose can perfectly well and with no logical strain be accomplished by the absolute notion of truth. This idea requires clarification, however, in view of various objections that might be thought to challenge it, along with the law of non-contradiction, of which it is a corollary. It might, for example, be objected that there is a familiar class of sentences whose truth clearly *does* change with time, place, or person, e.g.:

(i)   Today is Sunday.
(ii) This city has exactly two daily newspapers.
(iii) I am a vegetarian.

Clearly, neither (i), nor (ii), nor (iii) is invariably true or false. Sentence (i) is true only on Sundays and false every other day; (ii) is true only in such cities as have exactly two daily newspapers and false in every other city; (iii) is true only when said by a vegetarian and false when said by any non-vegetarian.

In reply, it may be pointed out that these sentences are all incomplete or indeterminate, none making a definite assertion, for their grammatical subjects have no fixed references. How can any of these sentences be evaluated for truth when it is not clear to what thing its attribute is purportedly being applied? Suppose one said "X is a Democratic candidate for President." Would this utterance be anything more than the schema of a statement? Clearly this schema has no fixed truth value but may be transformed into an indefinite number of sentences with fixed truth values by replacing the variable "X" by a name or description, or by prefixing the whole by "Every X is such that" or "There is an X such that." The absolute theory of truth is not a denial that schemata are thus variable in respect of truth, but schemata should not be confused with determinate sentences.

It may be granted that (i), (ii), and (iii) are in one respect more determinate than schemata with variables such as "X," "Y," etc. The word "today," for example, although it varies in reference (as does "X" under suitable supplementation as we have seen), nevertheless has particular occurrences, each with a definite reference fixed by its temporal context (without any supplementation), unlike "X." That is to say, when a particular speaker assertively utters the words, "Today is Sunday," "Today" refers to the day on which this particular utterance itself falls. Though the abstract word "Today" may vary in reference from occurrence to occurrence, this variability is constrained, for each occurrence, by a general relation that identifies its reference with its occurrence time. Analogously, "This city" refers, on each occasion of its utterance, to the city in which the utterance occurs. This general relation precludes the limitless variability enjoyed by the variable "X" and restricts the reference of "This city," on each occasion, to the city of its occurrence. Finally, the word "I" refers, on each occasion of its utterance, to the utterer; such relation limiting its complete variability (unlike the case of "X") while allowing a range of variability within its special limits.

Nevertheless, the forms (i), (ii), and (iii), considered apart from the contexts of their particular utterances, do not succeed in making assertions any more than do schemata. However, as soon as the relevant contexts of their several utterances are taken into account, not only do the purported references of each utterance become determinate, but the truth-value of each utterance is fixed. The utterance, on a given occasion, of "Today is Sunday" is thus true or false absolutely, depending on the day of the week referred to by the utterance of "Today" on that occasion, and it matters not that an utterance of the same form of words may have a differing truth value on a different occasion when its "Today" utterance may vary relevantly in its reference.

It is worth noting that variable indexical or indicator words, such as "today," "this," "I," etc., may be supplanted entirely by non-indexical expressions with definite references. In this way a fixed truth value is attained which is preserved even when the same form of words is repeated in differing circumstances. When "President Truman is a Democrat" thus replaces President Truman's own utterance, "I am a Democrat," its truth is fixed, not only as a particular utterance but as a repeatable form of words; it has been freed from dependence on the varying contexts of "I" in determining its reference.[8]

5. Transparency, Tarski, and Carnap

A peculiarity of the notion of absolute truth is that it seems to be totally *transparent*, that is, to add nothing to the sentence said to be true.

"That's true" is, like "Yes," just a mode of assent to a sentence understood in context, a way of re-asserting it without literally repeating it. Similarly, the prefix "It is true that," attached to a sentence, or the predicate "is true," appended to the name or description of the sentence, asserts nothing more nor less than does the sentence itself. The prefix "It is true that" seems to be just a device to add emphasis to the sentence in question, while the predicate "is true," attached to its name or description, affirms nothing other than what the sentence itself affirms, the predication and the sentence of which truth is predicated being true together or false together. The truth attribution is thus itself correct if, and only if, its affirmation is equivalent to that of the very sentence in question. The same conditions that make the latter sentence true also make the truth attribution itself true.

The transparency of absolute truth has occasionally been thought puzzling, raising the natural question as to what affirmations of such truth accomplish. Are they simply redundant, serving no useful purpose, hence dispensable? Alfred Tarski's "semantic conception of truth"[9] provides an account that explains the function of such affirmations while preserving their transparency and differentiating them from relative notions of confirmation and the like. He calls his conception semantic since it treats the attribution of "true" to certain sentences as serving to link these sentences to the attributions made by the sentences themselves—semantics having to do with the relations between language and its objects.

Tarski's inspiration is Aristotle's doctrine: "To say of what is that it is not, or of what is not that it is, is false, while to say of what is that it is or of what is not that it is not, is true." Tarski takes this idea to have a popular modern formulation in the statement, "The truth of a sentence consists in its agreement with (or correspondence to) reality." His proposed criterion is intended to give a precise restatement of the underlying idea, eliminating the vague reference to reality. He illustrates the criterion by pointing out the equivalence between the sentence, "Snow is white," and the quite different sentence, "'Snow is white' is true," the former referring to snow while the latter refers to a sentence. Though these sentences are quite different, the one is true if, and only if, the other is true; they are in this respect equivalent, although clearly non-identical. Tarski claims that this particular equivalence must hold under any adequate definition of truth.

Generalizing, he now formulates his semantic criterion as requiring, for every such definition, that all equivalences of the following form must hold:

"_____" is true if, and only if, _____,

it being understood that both blanks are filled by the same sentence, under a fixed interpretation, belonging to the language of the formula itself. It is clear that this criterion is not a device for generating mere tautologies, for the left blank, framed by quotation marks, forms a name of whatever sentence is inserted in it while the right blank does not, making no reference at all to the sentence quoted in the left blank. As a whole, the criterion thus serves to relate the truth of the sentence quoted on the left to the independent condition stated by the sentence on the right. (For the use of quotation marks on the left, any other naming device may, moreover, be substituted, provided only that it names the sentence in the blank on the right.) The entire formula represents Tarski's semantic criterion of truth.

This criterion relates the quotation of a sentence to the sentence quoted, the former mentioning the latter. But, as just noted, quotation is not the only way to mention a sentence; one can, for instance, single out a sentence by description, viz. "The second full sentence on page 297 of Volume 8 of the Britannica," and go on to assert that that sentence is true, without even knowing in what form of words the mentioned sentence consists. Yet the attribution of truth to that sentence is intended to be understood as equivalent to the mentioned sentence itself.

The criterion is therefore clearly not a definition of truth, because it is insufficiently general, incapable of eliminating every context of "is true" by a designated equivalent. Further, the criterion formula is not a full sentence at all but only a schema, containing blanks which, when filled, yield a limitless supply of specific sentences, none therefore fit to serve as a definition. Yet the criterion represents a condition of adequacy that must, according to Tarski, be satisfied by any correct definition of truth: Any such definition, that is, needs to be such that every sentence formed in accord with the criterion formula follows from the definition. It is not necessary here to go into Tarski's own definition, as distinct from his criterion, for the criterion itself suffices to show the independence of truth from confirmation, thus exhibiting the force of the absolute conception of truth, which it represents. Further, in showing the attribution of truth to a sentence to be tantamount to, though not identical with, the sentence itself, the criterion accounts for the transparency earlier discussed, in a way that occasions no logical difficulties.

It should be especially noted that the criterion offers no method for deciding whether or not to affirm the sentence in the first place; it does not tell us, for example, if snow is indeed white or not. It says only that "whenever we assert or reject this sentence, we must be ready to assert or reject the correlated sentence . . . '"Snow is white" is true.'" Since true sentences are, moreover, indefinitely varied, is it any wonder that a unitary method for *ascertaining* truth is a difficult, likely an impossible, objective? In any case, the criterion is itself sufficient to show that there is no more mystery in truth than in the various sentences themselves asserted to be true. As W. V. Quine has remarked, "Attribution of truth in particular to 'snow is white', for example, is every bit as clear to us as attribution of whiteness to snow."[10] To put the point metaphorically, truth is a semantic reflection of the references of our multifarious descriptions themselves, and the absoluteness of truth mirrors the intelligibility of such descriptions as they stand. The discussion of truth in particular cases of course presupposes a particular language. But the contrast of absolute with relative truth holds within whatever language parameter is pertinent.

If we use "white" solely as a categorical predicate, the question, "Is snow white?" does not admit the further query, "White for whom?" If, however, we use the relative predicate "white for" to distinguish certain experimental subjects from others, the question, "Is snow white for Jones?" is allowable but does not itself permit the further question, "White for Jones for whom?"

Rudolf Carnap, building on Tarski's criterion, shows the difference between absolute truth and confirmation, and the immunity of truth to objections against certainty. Carnap's argument, in slightly altered form, may be presented by reference to the following three sentences:[11]

(i) The substance in the vessel at time *t* is alcohol.
(ii) "The substance in the vessel at time *t* is alcohol" is true.
(iii) X believes (confirms, accepts) now, that the sentence, "The substance in the vessel at time *t* is alcohol" is true.

Following Tarski, (i) holds if, and only if, (ii) does. But the same can clearly not be said of (i) and (iii). For the vessel may contain alcohol at *t*, while X believes (confirms, accepts) now that the sentence "The substance in the vessel at time *t* is alcohol" is false. Conversely, X may hold the sentence in question to be true even though the vessel does not contain alcohol at *t* but rather water. It follows that (ii) also diverges from (iii), for (ii) holds just in those conditions under which (i) does. Thus, the sentence, "The substance in the vessel is alcohol," may well be true but not believed by X to be true, and vice versa. Truth is therefore one thing and being believed, accepted, or confirmed as true at a given time is quite another.

So far, we have seen how Tarski's criterion dissolves the puzzle of truth's transparency by distinguishing identity from equivalence, thus eliminating the charge of redundancy and showing the special force of truth attributions, such attributions being equivalent to, but non-identical with, the sentences to which attributions are made. We have further seen Carnap's argument, distinguishing truth from belief, confirmation, and the like. The net effect of these two results is to recognize that absolute truth is not simply eliminable as otiose, nor is it reducible to such relative notions as those of belief, confirmation, verification, justification, or the like.

6. Truth and Certainty

A third challenge to absolute truth remains to be considered, one that has had wide support among scientists, philosophers, and laymen alike. This challenge rests on the argument that since the absolute truth or falsity of any empirical sentence can never be decided with certainty, the absolute notion of truth should be abandoned, for scientific purposes at least. To this challenge, Carnap responds by granting that the certainty referred to is indeed out of the question. But does it follow that truth is therefore inadmissible? Such an inference apparently hinges on the principle "A term (predicate) must be rejected if we can never decide with certainty, for any given instance, whether or not the term applies." But this principle, argues Carnap, "would lead to absurd consequences." For if we cannot decide the application of "true" in sentence (ii) above, with certainty, then, by the same token, we cannot decide the application of "alcohol" in sentence (i) with certainty; conversely, if we could be certain about the term "alcohol" in (i), we could equally be certain about "true" in (ii). If we follow the above principle in rejecting "true," we shall also need to reject all empirical terms as well.

The principle in question may then be replaced by a weaker version, as follows: "A term (predicate) is a legitimate scientific term . . . if, and only if, a sentence applying the term to a given instance can possibly be confirmed to at least some degree." This version no longer has the absurd consequences of its predecessor. Clearly, it legitimizes "alcohol," but also, by the same token, it legitimizes "true." The large consequence of this argument is that even if we totally reject certainty, we are not compelled to reject absolute truth, which has, as we have already shown, important independent functions of its own.

One further function deserving special mention here is to serve as a necessary condition of knowing, as traditionally conceived. According to this conception, if we say that someone knows that *P*, then "*P*" is affirmed by us to be true, in the absolute sense of the term. To be sure, we cannot claim certainty for this affirmation; our knowledge attributions are not infallible. Any of these attributions may turn out to be mistaken, but they are no worse than any of our other attributions, all of which are fallible. If we allow ourselves to make other such attributions, how can we deny ourselves the right to make knowledge attributions in particular?

Since we cannot, in general, be obliged to do what is impossible for us to do, we cannot be obliged to attain certainty in any of our assertions. We can, however, be expected to fashion our attributions in accordance with the best evidence available to us, to treat them as open to criticism and as vulnerable always to revision pending the emergence of convincing contrary evidence. The prospect of such future revision, presently contemplated, is indeed what makes our current attributions incapable of absolute assurance. But this hypothetical prospect is no reason for controverting whatever preponderant evidence is available to us now, or for refraining from judgment altogether. When and if sufficient contrary evidence emerges, we shall then have good reason to revise our present judgments but, meanwhile, the mere fact that contrary evidence may emerge later constitutes no cause for present revision. Knowledge attributions, in sum, are no different from other attributions in respect of certainty. Our job is not to judge the truth infallibly but to estimate the truth responsibly. Having, to the best of our ability, determined a given sentence to be justified by the totality of our available evidence, we may then, with an untroubled conscience, affirm it to be true.

7. Sentences as Truth Candidates

We noted earlier that interactional justification is applicable not only to sentences, that is, bearers of truth value, but also to acts, rules, laws, and other entities as well. Here we propose to attend first to sentences as truth candidates, leaving the consideration of other subjects of justification for later. This plan brings us face to face with a new question: Which sentences are, in fact, truth candidates? The answer may seem obvious, since sentences are defined by the presumed language of the sentences in question, i.e., by its lexicon and grammar. However, the seeming obviousness of this answer is an illusion, for not all the grammatical sentences of a language have truth value.

First, interrogative and imperative sentences need to be excluded, incapable as they are of being affirmed as true or false, or construed as objects of belief. It should also be noted that the notion of truth is connected with that of evidence, as is illustrated by the two cases just considered, neither questions nor commands construable as having evidence either for or against them. Now aside from these exclusions, certain indicative sentences are controversial because of lexical items they contain, certain thinkers barring sentences using them from counting as truth candidates, while other thinkers pose no such barriers. Examples are sentences using ethical or moral terms or those expressing aesthetic or other forms of judgment; notable here is the difference between emotive and cognitive theorists, the former denying and the latter affirming the receptivity of such sentences to the notion of truth.

8. Theoretical Terms

Within science, a major controversy has divided thinkers over the status of so-called theoretical terms which, as distinct from the qualitative terms descriptive of our ordinary experience, increasingly serve to integrate scientific systems and enhance their predictive, explanatory, and practical powers. Thus, certain thinkers have refused to acknowledge the existence of atomic or other postulated particles beneath the level of observability, despite their recognition of the practical and theoretical virtues of such postulation. Another celebrated example is the infinitesimal, ingredient in the calculus, itself a powerful instrument in the science of mechanics, but logically self-contradictory in requiring the existence of instantaneous accelerations.[12]

Those skeptics who have balked at affirming the truth value of sentences with the suspect terms have continued to rely on them, hoping that an acceptable reduction would someday become available. A successful reduction was that of Weierstrass, who paraphrased the infinitesimal in terms of the concept of limits. But in unreduced cases, the skeptics have often understood apparent indicative sentences rather as mere instruments of science than as affirmations, helpful in calculation, prediction, and practical application, but lacking eligibility for truth.

9. Varieties of Instrumentalism

The minimal form of instrumentalism simply requires the use of other notions than those relating to truth in application to suspect sentences. Considering these sentences to be mere machinery, the minimal instrumentalist leaves suspect scientific formulations unchanged. Such an instrumentalist needs but to alter operative attitudes toward them, refraining from characterizing them as truth vehicles and relying instead on such substitute epithets as "useful," "interesting," "holds," "fails," etc., for the suspect sentences, as needed.[13]

10. Pragmatism and Instrumentalism

Unlike instrumentalism, a pragmatic approach accepts theoretical formulations in science as truth vehicles, making no distinction within the corpus of science between sentences aspiring to truth and those functioning merely as symbolic instruments. In following this course, pragmatists have the advantage of simplifying procedural matters, whereas instrumentalists, though complicating their internal syntactic structures, have the advantage of preserving a critical stance toward the scientific notions they use. This critical stance is useful for science itself, as illustrated by the Weierstrass example earler cited. Nevertheless, since the minimal instrumentalism we have been considering uses the extant formulations of science as does pragmatism, the two positions have often been confused, the opposition between them frequently deemed to lack substance.

Stronger versions of instrumentalism have also been proposed, distinguished by their pursuit of programs for eliminating suspect sentences from prevailing scientific formulations. As distinct from minimal instrumentalism, these versions are eliminatist, intending to purge suspect sentences from extant science while retaining the utility heretofore afforded by these sentences.[14] We need not here discuss these eliminatist versions in technical detail. It suffices to say that the focus on sentences as truth vehicles requires, for its application to particular bodies of science or other claimants to knowledge, decisions as to which sentences will be treated as such.

Having now, let us suppose, decided on the sentences to be treated as truth vehicles within our language, and having, further, judged a number of these sentences to be true, we hold them nevertheless vulnerable to withdrawal. But we continue to recognize their systematic import, that is, the fact that they are not judged merely distributively, one by one, but as elements of collectivities aspiring to higher credibility than their rivals. Although subjected to empirical test as individual units, they are ultimately judged by the scope of their interconnections with other such units as members of systems in process.

11. Systems, Simplicity, Reduction

Systems in science normally do not simply incorporate raw, pre-systematically credible sentences taken as true, for they may conflict with other such sentences equally taken as true, judged individually. Systems stretch, smooth, trim, and approximate, in order to facilitate a consistent and maximal community of pre-systematic sentences with high credibility as a community. In this process, systems tend to develop a common language. They also press for increased precision of statement, suitable criteria of judgment, introduction of measurement where possible, and, lastly, new theoretical matter promising to advance the integration of the mass of sentences involved. In the manner of Peirce's abduction discussed earlier, a proposed new theory may garner support from the scattered, initially credible sentences that logically follow from it, but, more importantly, from the access of credibility gained for the community of sentences by its introduction. Such new theories may also lend individual sentences further support by explaining them while doing the same for a host of their kin near and far.

Systems perform a number of important related functions. They articulate connections among sentences otherwise considered solely as individuals, in the process often discovering commonalities among sentences considered denizens of alien realms. A celebrated example is the replacement of Aristotle's division between terrestrial and celestial motion by the uniform mechanics of Newton. Another, discussed earlier, is the way in which modern evolutionary systems have unearthed hitherto unsuspected links among the different species, thus increasing both their explanatory power and their credibility. The wider such *interconnection* extends, the more it adds to the integration of, and support for, a given system.

Interconnection is a corollary of *simplicity*. The simpler a system, the fewer are its conceptual assumptions and the fewer the independent assertions it harbors among its given statements, hence the greater the integration of its parts. A particular mass of sentences is the simpler as its constituent predicates are increasingly connected through definition, and its sentences increasingly connected through logical derivation. A particular form of simplification has been widely discussed under the label of *reduction*, referring to cases in which independent systems are newly interconnected in wholesale fashion through definition or derivation.

A much discussed and controversial example is the proposed reduction of mathematics to logic, through suitable definitions of mathematical terms in exclusively logical ones, in the manner exemplified by Whitehead's and Russell's *Principia Mathematica*, mentioned earlier (see Chapter 1, "Justification"). This proposal, exemplary in its specificity and clarity, is controversial because of differences over the content of the logic assumed, specifically as to whether set theory is to be considered part of logic, or not.

Another much discussed example is the reduction of thermodynamics to statistical mechanics and the kinetic theory of gases.[15] Ernest Nagel's analysis of this example illustrates his interpretation of a major sort of reduction in science. According to this interpretation, such reduction involves derivation of the laws of the science to be reduced, from the principles of the reducing science, as well as the connection of terms of the reduced science to those of the reducing science sufficient to enable the derivation to go forward.[16]

The interconnections just discussed heighten a system's credibility, hence its relative support. To revert to Peirce's metaphor of a scientific system as a cable of interwoven slender threads, the tighter the weave the fewer the loose ends and the dangling threads—and the stronger the cable. Or, to change the figure in accordance with a suggestion of Russell, a bridge gains support not merely from the perpendicular posts upon which its respective sections rest but also from the transverse rods attaching these posts to one another. The more support is diffused throughout the structure, the stronger it is; the more credible if we are dealing with a structure of theory.[17]

Reduction is difficult to achieve. If we take as our two exemplary cases those mentioned previously, such achievement presupposes perfect clarity as to the sentences to be reduced and the sentences to which they are to be reduced, the definitions to be employed or auxiliary principles, if any, that may be used in connecting reduced terms to reducing terms, as well as clarity with respect to the logical principles empowering required derivations of reduced from reducing sentences with the help of definitions and allowable auxiliary principles.

Because reduction in the manner of such exemplary cases is so difficult, it is rare, and well-known attempts have foundered through failure to satisfy one or another desideratum. Thus, phenomenalism, the attempt to reduce physical statements to phenomenal ones, as well as its obverse, physicalism, both do not succeed for lack of clarity regarding any of the desiderata. Another flawed attempt is methodological individualism, aimed at reducing social or political science to psychological sentences concerning individual persons.

The failure of given programs of reduction is by no means a failure in the generic sense, a total loss or waste of time. Like the falsification of a scientific hypothesis, which offers new and often significant knowledge, stimulating new leads and spawning alternative hypotheses, a reduction failure is instructive in analogous ways, enabling us to discard fruitless strategies and move on in other directions. As with scientific falsifications too, reduction failures offer the opportunity to conduct detailed post mortems to explain these failures and thus to gain new understandings.

Other reactions to failures of reduction programs are not so happy. One such reaction is a sour grapes response: "We didn't need the exemplary form of reduction anyway; we can achieve reductions simply by weakening exemplary requirements." Thus phenomenalism succeeds after all since all our physical knowledge rests on observation, and all observation is phenomenal. Conversely, physicalism in fact succeeds since everything we know about mental phenomena is ascribable to living organisms, that is, to certain physical objects. And methodological individualism is successful too in reducing social science to psychology because the nations, states, and cultures treated by the former are composed of nothing but individual human beings. We have here what has been termed "ontological reduction" rather than reduction in the exemplary form we have discussed, and the weakening of the latter's requirements consists in omitting the derivation of the reduced sentences from those of the reducing ones.

The problem is that ontological reduction, so called, is no reduction at all, effecting no simplification in the prevailing body of sentences with which we started. The ontologically reduced sentences are not eliminable in favor of the reducing ones. They remain in our system, unintegrated danglers to be accommodated as before, adding no strength or support beyond what was available earlier. To add insult to injury, the term "ontological reduction" invites us to think that it names a species of genuine reduction, authorizing us to suppose, absurdly, that psychology has been reduced to physics as have botany and linguistics as well.

Another unhappy reaction to failures of reduction programs is the dialectical response: The acknowledged failure of a given program may well be thought to be merely temporary, to be overcome in the future by a successful program yet to be achieved. So far so good; such judgment is not in itself objectionable, being a mere expression of the faith that a genuine reduction exists. This faith may power laudable constructive efforts to find such a reduction. The dialectical response, on the other hand, powers no such efforts; instead, it goes up a semantic level and offers arguments purporting to show, or to deny, that a genuine reduction is sure to exist, or to speculate as to whether or not such a reduction is possible or likely. Oceans of philosophical ink have been spilled in efforts to make the existence of such reductions credible or not—short of producing one—and additional oceans spilled in speculating as to the possibility of such reduction.

An example of a dialectical discussion pitched at too rarefied a level to lend itself to decision is a recent debate over the so-called mind–body identity theory in a formulation of Herbert Feigl.[18] Acknowledging that "any detailed account of the psychological–physical identities is a matter for the future progress of psychophysiological research," Feigl nevertheless maintains that "it is plausible that only certain types of cerebral processes in some of their (probably configurational) aspects are identical with the experienced and acquaintancewise knowable raw feels." In Wilfrid Sellars' summary, "[Feigl's] claim [which Sellars disputes] is that among the universals which would find expression in the predicates of a to be developed 'brain state' theory, some are identical with 'raw feel' universals."[19] To argue over what sorts of predicates would be included in an unknown theory of the future resembles the stereotyped issue of angels dancing on the head of a pin. As Karl Popper has rightly maintained, if there is any area in which the predictive confidence of science falters, it is in forecasting its own future vocabulary and theories, for if it could foretell them, it would have them.[20] Even if we could somehow foretell certain reductive features of future science, we would have advanced not one whit toward the goal of a genuine reduction. The illusion of such advance is indeed nothing but a mirage, to be resisted while holding fast to the requirements of a genuine reduction, which simplifies, integrates, and strengthens a theoretical cluster of our beliefs.

We spoke earlier of the mass of beliefs with which we started, and which are revised in the course of reflective experience in pursuit of an increased credibility of the total mass. It is now important to note that the mass does not comprise a single theory or theoretical cluster. It is, rather, a miscellany, an aggregate of all our beliefs, true and false, general and particular, momentous and trivial. Within this aggregate, there are pockets of systematic organization, comprising sentences sharing basic vocabularies and logical cross connections. These pockets are typified most clearly by scientific fields or areas of theory. It is such pockets that I call clusters, an admittedly vague and variable designation, but sufficient for present purposes. It is clusters that are likely candidates for reductions that may integrate and strengthen them, tending toward an increased credibility of their containing mass.

12. Crises in Science

It is evident why reduction is a prime desideratum of scientific inquiry, pruning the relevant clusters of extraneous assumptions, hence enhancing the support of those that remain. The pursuits of economy, simplicity, and elegance are embodied in the selfsame drive toward reduction. It is also understandable that unsuccessful attempts at reduction are often felt to be scientific failures even, in certain cases, described as crises. Outstanding modern examples include hitherto unsuccessful attempts to reconcile classical mechanics with quantum theory, and failure as yet to find a way of bringing together in one theoretical framework the four fundamental physical forces: the strong force, the weak force, electromagnetism, and gravitation. That it is supremely desirable for such attempts eventually to succeed is not contested. But it is an overstatement to describe as a crisis of physics the failure as yet to solve the problem. The recent heated striving to achieve a solution through string notions, promising at last to produce a "theory of everything," is only the latest symptom of a skewed view of science.

Several recent writers have criticized string theories for failing to generate predictions capable of yielding empirical tests. But a more telling criticism points, first, to the variety and heterogeneity of the mass of beliefs from which scientific clusters take their beginnings as critical specializations. Even were all the beliefs of this mass minus the clusters set aside, the likelihood of a single theory encompassing the clusters alone is so remote as to be unworthy of consideration. The notion that the normal situation in science is a single comprehensive explanatory framework, lacking which it approximates a state of crisis, is wildly at odds with the facts. No matter how much science has ever thought itself able to explain, it has, in every period of its growth, lacked explanations for an infinite number of facts. In a metaphor of Bertrand Russell's, the explained facts known to mankind are comparable to the contents of a single shaky rowboat, while those unexplained outstrip the capacity of all the earth's seas. The default position in science is a wide variety of beliefs and explanatory schemes characterizing extant clusters, rather than uniformity. Such variety betokens not crisis but normality.

13. Reduction and Expansion

It is certainly evident that the urge to reduce is a master motive in scientific research, reflecting the methodological goal of simplification. It is further apparent that projecting this goal to the limit leads us to imagine a state in which everything is reduced by a single theory, the supposed ideal of science to the pursuit of which all research efforts are to be bent. Reduction is, however, not the only ideal animating scientific research and advance, although it is one moment of this process. Another moment is expansion, powered by the urge to explore regions beyond the reach of extant clusters altogether. Reduction simplifies and conserves; expansion explores and complicates. The result, whenever we examine science in any given period, is plain for all who have eyes to see: It is science as an aggregate of diverse clusters, each of which is a product of critical attempts to honor demands for clarity, credibility, and simplicity, as well as to subject its claims to logic and empirical test. What relates these clusters is a common adherence to such demands, expressing primary scientific values. But the variation among clusters is rather a matter of conceptual differences, enabling the formation of sentence groups lacking apparent syntactic or semantic kinship.

The clusters of science change in character and range from one period to the next, but the overall pattern of value commonality across clusters combined with conceptual variation between them persists throughout every period we may select. Extant clusters exhibit the effects both of new growth and of simplification; of expansion as well as reduction. These complementary moments in the career of science of course do not appear in sequence for the whole group of clusters. New growths of science do not await the conclusion of simplifications in process; they arise in certain areas simultaneously or not, with reductions elsewhere in a continual but irregular development. The idea of a theory of everything is the vision of a future in which science has ceased to grow, its forward movement come to a dead halt, having no new worlds to conquer. This view of a static paradise awaiting the demise of science is at odds with everything we know of its history, ignoring its expansive moment altogether while exaggerating its reductive moment beyond all recognition. Unless by a theory of everything is meant a theory of everything within a clearly restricted domain, the idea is a mirage.

Notes

1   W. V. Quine, *From a Logical Point of View* (Cambridge, MA: Harvard University Press, 1961), pp. 134–35.

2   W. V. Quine, *The Ways of Paradox* (New York: Random House, 1966), ch. 1.

3   William James, *Pragmatism* (New York: Longmans, Green, 1907), p. 218.

4   Ibid., p. 200.

5   My discussion in the following three sections draws from chapter 2 of my *Conditions of Knowledge* (Chicago: Scott Foresman, 1965, and University of Chicago Press, 1978, 1983).

6   See A. Koyré, "Galilée et l'Expérience de Pise," *Annales de L'Université de Paris* (1937): 441–53, and Herbert Butterfield, *The Origins of Modern Science* (New York: Macmillan, paperback edition, 1960), pp. 81–82.

7   James, op. cit., pp. 223–24.

8   On indicator words, see Nelson Goodman, *The Structure of Appearance*, 3rd ed. (Boston: Reidel, 1977), pp. 261–75.

9   Alfred Tarski, "The Semantic Concept of Truth: and the Foundations of Semantics," *Philosophy and Phenomenological Research* 4 (1944); see also *Readings in Philosophical Analysis*, H. Feigl and W. Sellars, eds. (New York: Appleton-Century-Crofts, 1949), pp. 52–54. See also W. V. Quine, *From a Logical Point of View*, op. cit., ch. 7.

10 Quine, ibid., p. 138.

11 Rudolf Carnap, "Truth and Confirmation," in Feigl and Sellars, op. cit., p. 54.

12 On the problem of infinitesimals and Weierstrass' solution, see W. V. Quine, *Word and Object* (Cambridge, MA: Technology Press of MIT and New York: John Wiley and Sons, 1960), pp. 248–51.

13 See Israel Scheffler, *The Anatomy of Inquiry* (Indianapolis: Hackett, 1981), pp. 186–88.

14 A discussion of several such eliminatist programs is contained in Scheffler, ibid., pp. 188–222.

15 Ernest Nagel, *The Structure of Science* (New York and Burlingame: Harcourt, Brace & World, 1961), ch. 11, esp. pp. 338–66.

16 Ibid.

17 Russell, op. cit., pp. 395–96.

18 Herbert Feigl, "The Mental and the Physical," in *Minnesota Studies in the Philosophy of Science*, vol. 2, H. Feigl, M. Scriven, and G. Maxwell, eds. (Minneapolis: University of Minnesota Press, 1958), vol. 2, p. 457.

19 Wilfrid Sellars, "The Identity Approach to the Mind–Body Problem," in *Boston Studies in the Philosophy of Science*, R. S. Cohen and M. Wartofsky, eds. (New York: Humanities Press, 1965), p. 78.

20 K. Popper, *The Poverty of Historicism* (London: Routledge, 1961), ch. 7.

Chapter 3

Worlds

1. Philosophies of Truth

It is time to return to the subject of truth, specifically to address large philosophical approaches to it, having dealt earlier with certain analytical aspects of truth claims. We have, latterly, recounted Tarski's semantic conception, along with some of the details involved in its interpretation. Quine has dubbed Tarski's criterion a view of truth as disquotation, since it takes the attribution of truth to a quoted sentence in a language L to be equivalent to the bare sentence itself within L.[1] We have noted that the disquotational view falls short of a definition, offering a criterion only which, unlike a genuine definition, does not provide a way of eliminating the predicate "true" from every context in which it appears, e.g., one in which the purportedly true sentence is not quoted but is otherwise uniquely specified. Yet it provides a condition of adequacy that, as Tarski claims, every definition must meet. He also constructs a genuine definition of truth for formalized languages, while for general use he supplies only his semantic criterion.

Philosophers have traditionally attempted to define truth, seeking to explicate the nature of truth in some general formula. One school of thought (the realistic) has identified truth with correspondence to reality; another (the idealistic), with coherence of a totality of beliefs. In the debates between these rivals, stock arguments have recurred repeatedly, without resolving the rivalry between them. The realistic school has failed to explain either the reality to which it purports to refer or the correspondence relation it invokes. The idealistic school has failed to say how one coherent totality is to be singled out as true as against an infinite number of others inconsistent with the first. Modern philosophical schools have made valiant attempts to overcome the rifts between realistic and idealistic tendencies in their own views of truth without, however, achieving consensus.

The logical positivist school harbored an early inconclusive debate between two of its leading figures, Moritz Schlick, who defended a realistic interpretation, and Otto Neurath, who argued for an idealistic view.[2] Pragmatic philosophers have shared a broad agreement in their understanding of meaning, but have shown deep divisions in their interpretations of truth.

We have already discussed William James, who treated truth as a mutable property, holding it to be made in the course of experience, and viewing it as a collective name for verification processes. C. S. Peirce, on the other hand, diverged strongly from James, calling the mutability of truth "a seed of death" that has been allowed to infect pragmatism, a philosophy "so instinct with life."[3] Both Peirce and James, moreover, drew their inspiration from science as opposed to dogmatism and upheld the doctrine that Peirce dubbed fallibilism.[4] How, given his fallibilism, was Peirce nevertheless able to defend the immutability of truth? We earlier noted a distinction between absolute truth and certainty, which allows attacks on the latter to leave the former intact. Failing to acknowledge such distinction, James denies absolute truth as well as certainty, while Peirce, distinguishing the two, denies certainty while defending absolute, that is to say, immutable truth. Fallibilism thus unites these two thinkers while the interpretation of truth divides them.

Peirce does not simply affirm truth's immutability, however; he proceeds to offer his own general view of it as "the opinion which is fated to be ultimately agreed to by all who investigate."[5] This notion of truth is an ideal and absolute one: the truth is not relative to time, person, or circumstance; it is the fixed limit toward which inquiry tends.[6] Now, in an ironic twist, John Dewey seems to have misconstrued Peirce's conception of truth in the very process of declaring that his own definition, in terms of "warranted assertibility," is in agreement with it.[7] For such assertibility is clearly relative to time, person, and circumstance, in stark contrast with Peirce's absolute notion of truth as "the opinion . . . fated to be ultimately agreed to by all who investigate."

Now Peirce's view of truth cannot of course be taken seriously as a literal appeal to fate. Nor can ultimate agreement, however achieved, serve as a marker of truth here and now. Useless as a criterion, it provides no clarification but only an illusion. The suggestive idea of truth as permanence of belief is consonant with Peirce's view of inquiry as arising from doubt and ending with the settlement of belief. For a permanent belief is presumably intended as one never beyond a certain moment ever again vulnerable to doubt or replacement. But such permanence of belief, like ultimacy of agreement, is totally beyond service as a criterion of truth, for it does not reveal itself at any give time.

A treatment of truth in terms of permanence is suggested in Nelson Goodman's subtle discussion in his *Ways of Worldmaking*. "Although," he says, "we can never establish permanence of an object or material, we can establish durability in varying degrees short of permanence. Likewise, although we can never establish total and permanent credibility, we can establish strength and durability in varying degrees short of that. Shall we then identify unattainable total and permanent credibility with unattainable truth?" This proposal runs into the objection that total and permanent credibility might fasten on a falsehood, thus diverging from the truth. Here, Goodman suggests that any such divergence could not matter to us at all. We might then surrender truth in favor of total and permanent credibility, "which though equally unattainable is explicable in terms of what is attainable, just as permanence is explicable in terms of durability."[8]

This view is not presented by Goodman as his own, but rather as one alternative he discusses on the way to his own proposal of rightness as an overarching category subsuming truth along with other features relevant to assessing variant "versions" both in the sciences and the arts. Such versions, he holds, may be equally right though conflicting, determining conflicting worlds along with the versions we have created.

2. Operationism and Truth

Before considering the larger topic of worldmaking, we may note, in passing, Goodman's remark that "in the absence of any definitive and informative characterization, we apply various tests that we check against each other and against a rough and partial antecedent classification of statements as true and false. Truth, like intelligence, is perhaps just what the tests test; and the best account of what truth is may be an 'operational' one in terms of tests and procedures used in judging it."[9] Apparently in this vein, his succeeding discussion of deductive and inductive validity makes un-self-conscious use of "truth" without definition or qualification.

This so-called operational attitude harks back to earlier papers of Goodman, in which he denies the need to seek "exact and inclusive definition" in certain difficult cases: "... the most that is required here is that there be an appreciable number of clear cases, and that anomalous and paradoxical cases can be dealt with by reasonable rules." And again, "No complete definition is needed. If the animal before us is clearly a polar bear, the question whether there are polar bears on our island is settled even though we neither know how to define 'polar bear' nor are sure whether it applies to certain other animals."[10] Is it possible then that the philosophical quest for a definition of truth is simply misguided, a mere pursuit of a will-o'-the-wisp?

A consideration favoring this possibility harks back to Tarski's semantic criterion, which shows the attribution of truth to a sentence to be equivalent to the sentence itself. Where the latter is clear to us, the truth attribution must be equally clear to us, consisting of a patently clear case, a positive item for an operational definition. As Carnap has further argued, to rule the truth predicate inadmissible because it cannot be applied with certainty would, absurdly, rule inadmissible every empirical predicate as well for the same reason. Conversely, to legitimize an empirical predicate because its application to cases is confirmable to some degree is to legitimize the truth predicate by the same token.

In effect, the truth predicate presents no special or unique problem as compared to other predicates of the language in question. Certainly, there are special restrictions on the use of this predicate to avoid well-known paradoxes of self-reference, such as the Liar. But having satisfied some such necessary restrictions (and having prepared to cope with further paradoxes if and as they come to light), we find the truth predicate no less clear than any other we are willing to accept for our independent descriptive purposes, even without the need for definition.

We need, of course, to recall that truth attributions, like any other, are couched in particular languages, and that what may be thought true is an inscription or utterance taken to belong to a given language under consideration. The descriptive predicates of a particular language, clear enough to enable "true" to serve well in that language may not be equally clear in another. "True in L" rather than "true" is the cross-linguistic truth predicate, with the language parameter made explicit.[11]

One cannot simply inspect reality and list the truths evident there; the listing is our own contribution, not explicit in the reality we inspect. Beyond the bare language, moreover, particular restrictions, conventions or modifications in the use of our predicates may be assumed for practical, theoretical, conventional, or simplifying purposes. Whether a particular descriptive account (in Goodman's terminology, "a version") is right or not depends then on its assumed language as well as on the interpretive constructions placed on its constituent descriptors. Different right world-versions, so understood, may not only appear to conflict; they may not be intertranslatable nor reducible, one to the other. The putative worlds they determine and to which they correspond are disparate; the picture they represent is that of a plural array.

Since, moreover, we can describe anything only by describing it, the condition we have limned is irremediable; we can neither confront reality neat nor find a way of coalescing all our credible world-versions into one. It would seem, therefore, that all our knowledge consists of fragmented bodies of description determined by versions we have ourselves fashioned or inherited. This conclusion seems innocent enough since our extant descriptions are indeed made up of linguistic elements we have stipulated to have referential force. It would be quite another matter, however, to suppose our versions to determine not only our descriptions but also the things to which they purport to refer.

Goodman, however, makes this leap. He writes, "Of course, we want to distinguish between versions that do and those that do not refer, and to talk about the things and worlds, if any, referred to; but these things and worlds and even the stuff they are made of—matter, anti-matter, mind, energy, or whatnot—are fashioned along with the things and worlds themselves."[12]

3. Version-Dependence

This position of Goodman's has occasioned a long-running controversy between Goodman and myself;[13] my view has been that "a version of our making may purport to be true; whether it succeeds or not goes beyond the bare making, which therefore does not determine its truth, if true, nor create either the objects of which it speaks or their alleged properties."[14]

Some of the murkiness that has beclouded this and related issues has its source in the notion of version-dependence. Goodman claimed that "although 'table' is different from tables, and 'constellation' different from constellations, still tables and constellations and all other things are version-dependent."[15] Yet, he has also asserted that "such version-dependence does not imply that versions make their worlds but only that they have worlds answering to them."[16] If this latter assertion is now juxtaposed to his earlier statement, ". . . when I say that worlds are made, I mean it literally. . . . Surely we make versions, and right versions make worlds. And, however distinct worlds may be from right versions, making versions is making worlds,"[17] we can hardly avoid the impression of outright inconsistency. If version-dependence were indeed understood not to imply that worlds are made by (right) versions, but only that they "answer to them," the relativistic sting would be removed from such dependence. We would then, however, need to surrender the statement that "right versions make worlds," literally, in order to avoid self-contradiction. On the other hand, if we were to continue to affirm the latter statement while giving up the statement that ". . . version-dependence does not imply that versions make their worlds but only that they have worlds anwering to them," the relativistic sting would remain.[18]

Now Goodman himself does not assist us in acknowledging the threat of inconsistency nor does he acknowledge the two opposite ways we have imagined as eliminating the threat. His official view seems to be that "we make versions, and right versions make worlds," a formula that underlies the description of his overall doctrine as "a radical relativism under rigorous restraints, that eventuates in something akin to irrealism."[19]

His rigorous restraints set him apart from subjectivism, as does his insistence on the distinction between the true and the false. But his irrealism separates him from realism, and his radical relativism removes him from espousing such metaphysical ultimacies as materialism, idealism, dualism, and the like. I have myself not been persuaded by Goodman's irrealism, as I have above expounded it. Rather than reviewing our various arguments on related issues, however, I here recount a couple of crucial points of controversy.

Goodman says, "We cannot find any world feature independent of all versions. Whatever can be said truly of a world is dependent on the saying—not that whatever we say is true but that whatever we say truly . . . is nevertheless informed by and relative to the language or other symbol system we use. No firm line can be drawn between world-features that are discourse-dependent and those that are not."

To this I answer, "The trouble with [Goodman's argument] is that it appeals to the notion of a feature. But what is a feature? I presume that, for a nominalist such as Goodman, features will not be properties or classes but terms or predicates, construed as, or constituted by, tokens of one or another sort. Then of course features will obviously be dependent on the saying—that is, brought forth by the process of token production. . . . However, whether a feature or predicate of our making is *null or not* is not in the same way dependent on the saying; whether a statement is true or not is, as Goodman agrees, independent of our saying. Thus if by a world-feature, Goodman means a feature that is not null in fact, then that any given feature *is* a world-feature is indeed independent of our version. Its status as a world-feature is *not* discourse dependent."[20]

In another exchange, Goodman says I am disturbed by his saying "that a term or picture or other version is ordinarily different from what it denotes and yet also that talk of worlds tends to be interchangeable with talk of right versions." My response: "I am in fact not at all disturbed by this sort of statement, the flavor of which has become widely familiar through Alfred Tarski's semantic criterion of truth. Thus Goodman writes, "A version saying that there is a star up there is not itself bright or far off, and the star is not made up of letters. On the other hand, saying that there is a star up there and saying that the statement, 'There is a star up there' is true amount, trivially, to much the same thing, even though the one seems to talk about a star and the other to talk about a statement."

Rather, what disturbs me is what Goodman has himself criticized, namely, "philosophers [who] sometimes mistake features of discourse for features of the subject of discourse." As he continues, "We seldom conclude that the world consists of words just because a true description of it does." And here I would add, "We seldom conclude that the world is made by us just because a true description of it is."[21]

4. Differences among Scientifically Oriented Philosophers

I want now to recall the philosophical associations of the notions of truth and reality. An item of knowledge must of course be true, so the familiar realist story runs and, to be true, it must comply with what Schlick calls the good old expression "agreement with reality."[22] How exactly to locate what he calls the "unshakeable point of contact between knowledge and reality" presents a critical problem on which several scientifically oriented philosophers have disagreed. Positivist thinkers such as Carnap and Schlick himself have been divided on the question, and pragmatist thinkers such as Peirce and James have also differed on this issue, although all these have taken science as exemplary in seeking knowledge by somehow confronting theory with observed reality.

The critical point for all such thinkers is that thought must be constrained by data external to if it is not to be arbitrary. We have earlier quoted the pragmatist C. I. Lewis, who declared that "Unless the content of knowledge is recognized to have a condition independent of the mind, the peculiar significance of knowledge is likely to be lost. For the purpose of knowledge is to be true to something which is beyond it. . . . It is a real act with a real purpose because it seeks something which it knows it may miss. If knowledge had no condition independent of the knowing act, would this be so?"[23]

Philosophical interpretations of the intimated relations between knowledge, truth, and reality have been too varied to detail here. Instead we will focus, to begin with, on two polar opposites, one interpretation offered by Peirce, another by Goodman, and then consider a third interpretation which I myself favor. All are insistent on distinguishing the true from the false and on relating thought to the world, or worlds.

Both Peirce and Goodman distance themselves from idealism and subjectivism, insisting that thought must abide by relevant objective criteria. But Peirce affirms one world not of our making, interpreting inquiry as converging on this one world, while Goodman denies altogether the supposition of one world, holding that it is we who make worlds by constructing many world-versions. Peirce's position is thus realistic and monistic, while Goodman's is irrealistic and pluralistic. The position I myself uphold differs from both of these in being *plurealistic*, that is, both realistic and pluralistic. I now consider these positions in order.

5. Monism, Pluralism, Plurealism

For Peirce, the "fundamental hypothesis" of the method of science is that "there are real things, whose characters are entirely independent of our opinions about them."[24] He also holds that "all the followers of science are fully persuaded that the processes of investigation, if only pushed far enough, will give one certain solution to each question to which they can be applied."[25] Elaborating his view, he declares that scientists "may at first obtain different results, but, as each perfects his methods and his processes, the results will move steadily together toward a destined center. . . . Different minds may set out with the most antagonistic views, but the progress of investigation carries them by a force outside of themselves to one and the same conclusion. This activity of thought by which we are carried, not where we wish, but to a foreordained goal, is like the operation of destiny. No modification of the point of view taken, no selection of other facts for study, no natural bent of mind even, can enable a man to escape the predestinate opinion. This great law is embodied in the conception of truth and reality. The opinion which is fated to be ultimately agreed to by all who investigate is what we mean by the truth, and the object represented in this opinion is the real. That is the way I would explain reality."[26]

The realism of this passage is evident in the view that science presupposes there being things whose characters are entirely independent of our opinions about them, entities resistant to our wishes and wills. The monism of the passage is implied by the notion that the results of science "move steadily together toward a destined center," a foreordained goal which no scientific investigator can escape, even by changing the subject. The convergence upon such a center is a progressive approximation to the truth, whose object is the real. "There is a general *drift* in the history of human thought," says Peirce, "which will lead to one general agreement, one catholic consent."[27]

Now the picturesque mention of a predestinate opinion embodying the truth and representing the real must be qualified by introducing reference to language. For true statements are constituents of diverse languages, each, together with its logic, embodying a peculiar grammar and lexicon. The scientific investigations peculiar to the special branches of science, though they may share a common grammatical and logical apparatus, are yet recognizable by their distinctive extra-logical lexicons. Such investigations follow increasingly separate courses; scientific results, rather than moving steadily toward a destined center, tend to ramify as they pursue increasingly different itineraries, bound by no antecedent restrictions on their operative categories. Compare, for example, the languages of economics, geology, psychiatry, botany, genetics, and linguistics.

Reduction, as a general strategy of science, is of course always relevant since it simplifies our theories and, to the extent it is achieved, increases

their credibility and hence our confidence in them. But the reductions that
have been widely considered successful have always been partial. The prospect of wholesale reductions that would reduce the total number of scientific specialties at a given time to any appreciable degree, much less to one,
is a fantasy of science fiction. Whatever tendency toward piecemeal reduction may occur is more than counterbalanced by the tendency toward the
invention of new scientific specialties.

Monism has nevertheless been upheld by various contemporary thinkers who have appealed to the supposed primacy of physics among all the
separate branches of scientific knowledge. All scientific disciplines are, in
their view, ultimately reducible to physics. The operative word here is
"ultimately," for it is evident that the de facto array of sciences shows no
such reducibility to the concepts and theories of current physics. Indeed,
the notion of physics is itself problematic since the vocabulary, resources,
and statements of physics are constantly absorbed in a flux of change. Nor
should reducibility be confused with ontological characterizability. The
morphemes and phonemes of linguistics may, for example, be understood
to be physical objects, but the terms "morpheme" and "phoneme" are not
definable in the current vocabulary of physics nor is linguistics, in general,
reducible to present-day physics.

With reducibility to current physics clearly out of the question, the idea
of reducibility to some unknown future physics becomes indeterminate.
And the weaker thesis of ultimate reducibility to some common but
unspecified science becomes utterly vacuous. The idea that there is one
ultimate theory or conceptual domain to be reckoned with is no better than
an article of faith to be redeemed at best in some far-off hypothetical future.
Such monism of science as more than a tale told by some philosophers is
clearly groundless.

Despite Peirce's general formulation of monism, earlier cited, he himself
goes on to uphold a more moderate version of monism, relativized to each
choice of scientific question. Such relative monism overlooks the fact that
permanently unassimilable answers may be given to the same question.
Further, the underlying idea of convergence of opinion toward a single
answer relative to a given question faces insuperable difficulties. Such convergence is conceived as reducing the initial variety of opinion in a process
of approximation to an ideal limit. But this notion of approximation,
although it may plausibly apply to the increasing precision of measurements—a process with which Peirce was thoroughly familiar—cannot generally be applied to scientific opinion as a whole, inclusive of theories. For,

as Quine has said, "The notion of limit depends on that of "nearer than," which is defined for numbers and not for thories."[28]

If one were to imagine each successive theory to be a closer approximation to the truth than its predecessors, one would be construing the whole series as defining a line leading to the end point of truth, each later theory positioned on the line and differing from the rest only in relative distance from this end point. Or, changing the figure, one would be supposing that each successive theory draws an ever tighter boundary around the truth, which has already been captured within the wider area circumscribed by the earlier theory. But science does not always thus respect its own past. It does not generally conserve the direction marked out by earlier theories and simply extend the received line. Nor does it always suppose the truth to lie within the area bounded by previous theories. Often it strikes out anew, denying earlier theories altogether and proposing fresh directions of interpretation and areas of research. It seems thus impossible to fit the process of theoretical change in science into the framework provided by convergence.

Such reflections have been pressed by several thinkers critical of naive conceptions of scientific progress. Of these thinkers, T. S. Kuhn has been the best known. He insists that scientific revolutions replace one dominant paradigm by another and do not simply elaborate or refine the former, adding more information within its scope and passing it on smoothly to the next. Science, according to this view, does not develop in a straight line, by accumulation, but rather by zigs and zags in revolutionary upheaval.[29]

It might be argued, in response, that if science as a whole does not develop by accumulation, it does not follow that there is nothing in science that accumulates. Experimental and observational knowledge does after all often accumulate and its numerical bases do tend to become ever more precise even though theoretical interpretations of such knowledge are not, in general, conserved. Thus, if we distinguish theoretical from experimental (or observational) knowledge, we would conclude that the latter, even if not the former, frequently grows by convergence.

It is true that recent critics have also tended to reject the very distinction between theoretical and experimental or observational knowledge upon which this proposal rests. However, they have found it very difficult not to replace it with parallel distinctions to the same purpose within their own frameworks. Thus, Kuhn himself says that scientists are reluctant to embrace a new paradigm unless, first, it seems "to resolve some outstanding and generally recognized problem that can be met in no other way," and second, it promises "to preserve a relatively large part of the concrete problem-solving ability that has accrued to science through its predecessors. . . . [N]ew paradigms . . . usually preserve a great deal of the most concrete parts of past achievements and they always permit additional concrete problem-solutions besides. . . ."[30]

Nevertheless, the limit interpretation we have been considering is still not persuasive. For it leaves the fact of non-cumulative theoretical change to be dealt with. Science does not in general proceed along a fixed theoretical line, its results converging "toward a destined center" which it ever more closely approximates. The theoretical agreements of one period are often uprooted and superseded by conflicting agreements at a later time. If the notion of convergence thus proves incapable of representing scientific change even in its attenuated form, realistic monism is doomed by failure of its monistic constituent.

6. Realism versus Irrealism

But what of realism? Does it follow that if monism goes, realism must also be abandoned? Many have drawn this conclusion, supposing that with monism surrendered, we have given up all thought of objects responsive to our inquiries and "entirely independent of our opinions about them." The result is a variant of radical constructivism, anti-realism, or what Goodman has called his own view, i.e., "irrealism." I now consider Goodman's outline of the latter position as argued in his book, *Ways of Worldmaking*.

He attacks two doctrines: (1) that there is one world, and (2) that worlds must be taken as independent of versions, neither identical with nor made by them. Indeed he says, "We make worlds by making versions," and, "For many purposes, . . . versions can be treated as our worlds." He thus defends *pluralism* but rejects *realism*. He assumes that realists must be monists; hence to reject monism is to deny realism. Realists he calls absolutists, and he largely has those reductionists in mind who argue that physics is the ultimate reducing basis for all sciences, or for all knowledge. Thus, a corollary of his pluralism is his rejection of the thesis of physical reducibility as well as the notion of ultimate reducibility to any common base. If worlds need not be construed as independent of versions, and if they cannot be reduced to a common base, a plurality of worlds is the result, each identical with or a product of some right version.

Do his arguments against reduction, which uphold his pluralism, also tell against a multiplicity of worlds independent of versions? In other words, is his assumption correct that realism implies monism? If not, there is room for a pluralistic realism, i.e., a view that agrees with him in rejecting the notion of one world, but disagrees with him in that it holds whatever worlds there are to be independent of their corresponding versions. Such a view would acknowledge a variety of unreduced domains of entities, for each of which there are credible versions short of certainty but commanding a greater or lesser degree of confidence. This is in fact the plurealism I am myself inclined to support.[31]

In my earliest comment on *Ways of Worldmaking*, I had noted that "world" as used in that book was ambiguous, at times applying to what were called "right world versions," at times applying to the things referred to by such versions. I continued by arguing that the claim that we make worlds can be true only for the "versional," but not the "objectual" interpretation of "worlds." Goodman had insisted, to the contrary, that, although we distinguish between versions that do and those that do not refer, the things referred to are fashioned along with the versions themselves.

My attitude from the outset was that "worldmaking" as a metaphor for version-making I could tolerate, but "worldmaking" as a literal claim to the making thereby of the objects of such versions I could not. I thought it obvious that we made the word "star," and equally obvious that we did not make the stars, concluding that, despite his insistence on being taken literally, Goodman's statement "we make worlds by making versions" must of course be taken as purely rhetorical. Yet, he continued, in further exchanges, to affirm his claim, "when I say that worlds are made, I mean it literally. . . . Surely we make versions, and right versions make worlds. And, however distinct worlds may be from right versions, making versions is making worlds."

Goodman allows that if all right versions were reduced to one and only one, that one might plausibly be regarded as the "only truth about the only world," but he firmly rejects the prospect of such reduction. Might one not expect, then, that with one world alone ruled out, the prospect of many such worlds remains open? Yet Goodman instead prefers to treat versions themselves as worlds, thus ignoring the possibility of a plurality of worlds discrete from versions and thereby rejecting realism as well as monism.

Why does he rule out realism, even in pluralist guise? He offers three arguments. One of these rests on the indispensability of frames of reference. He writes, "If I ask about the world, you can offer to tell me how it is under one or more frames of reference, but if I insist that you tell me how it is apart from all frames, what can you say?" He here rules out the case where no frames are involved. But this exclusion is consistent not only with irrealism but also with plurealism, which Goodman appears to acknowledge in admitting that you can indeed tell how the world is under one or more frames of reference.

A second argument rests on an analysis of comparison. "We cannot test a version by comparing it with a world undescribed, undepicted, unperceived," he writes. "While we may speak of determining what versions are right as 'learning about the world', 'the world' supposedly being that which all right versions describe, all we learn about the world is contained in right versions of it. . . . For many purposes, right world-descriptions . . . or just versions can be treated as our worlds." But Goodman's criticism of "the world" as purporting to refer to the common reference of all right versions does not, I believe, tell against worlds as respectively referred to by particular right versions. To give up the notion of learning about *the* world leaves us the option of saying that determining what versions are right is learning about worlds.

In yet a third argument, Goodman denies that there can be perception without conception: "predicates, pictures, other labels, schemata," he writes, "survive want of application, but content vanishes without form. We can have words without a world but no world without words or other symbols." I agree there is no perception without conception, yet I insist that there can be worlds without words or other symbols.

On the basis of perception and conception, we thus in fact postulate worlds prior to speech or other symbolic representations, by which the origins of symbolism itself, independently of our making, might be explained. If such worlds prior to symbols are postulated now, have they lacked form until the present postulation, when they sprang into being in the past, which is inconceivable, or did they pop into existence at the time of postulation, in which case they would be useless in their hypothetical explanatory function? Neither of these unpleasant alternatives precludes the existence of worlds without words or other symbols.

Now the pluralism I advocate does not imply that to every version there corresponds a world but only that to every true version there corresponds a world. To every version I take to be true, I assign a domain I hold to exist. For compatible yet mutually irreducible versions, their domains— worlds, if you wish—may or may not be discrete. In either case, their joint affirmation occasions no problem. When, however, we are confronted with incompatible but equally credible versions, we cannot affirm them both.

Goodman had discussed one such sort of case in *The Structure of Appearance*. One can, for example, systematically define points as intersections of lines or lines as collections of points, in either case preserving the preferred relations between them. Yet the two treatments cannot be merged. Both systems are correct but they cannot be adopted simultaneously. What to do? Goodman insists that a correlation established by systematic definition does not assert an identity but only something considerably weaker. What one system in effect says is that, for certain presumed purposes at hand, points need not be supposed non-identical with certain intersections of lines, while the other system says, similarly, that, for certain purposes, lines need not be supposed non-identical with collections of points. Thus, both systematizations are now seen to be compatible and the common domain of both is the domain consisting of points and lines.[32]

Goodman, however, cites an extreme case of conflict, in his *Ways of Worldmaking*, which does not appear to him amenable to analogous resolution. "The earth moves" and "the earth stands still" are, he argues, both true yet incompatible, hence they must, he concludes, be construed as "true in different worlds." He rejects a relativization, for example, "The earth moves relative to the sun but not relative to my garage," saying that "an astronomer can no more work with a neutral statement of relative motion than we can use a map without locating ourselves on it in finding our way around a city." But in saying that the sun but not the earth moves relative to my telescope, I have, it seems to me, located myself for the purpose of making astronomical observations. Alternatively, a contextualization similar to the lines-and-points case is available here as well, for example, taking "the earth moves" as "For the purposes at hand, it is best to take the earth as moving." If so, the statement again becomes compatible with "the earth stands still" under analogous interpretation.

Goodman's critical case against these two solutions leaves me unpersuaded. His own preferred solution of the problematic incompatibility as implying that the conflicting statements are true in different worlds makes sense to me only if by "worlds" he means "world-versions," that is, systems. If so, his solution is tenable as well, requiring only the reading of "worlds" as "world-versions," but such reading does nothing to clarify his insistence that we make not only versions but whatever they refer to, "and even the stuff they are made of—matter, anti-matter, mind, energy, or what-not . . . all fashioned along with the versions themselves."

I am, finally, doubtful that such reading accords with his intentions, since some of his statements imply that they do not, for example, "Although 'table' is different from tables, and 'constellation' different from constella-tions, still tables and constellations and all other things are version depen-dent." The point here seems to be that making a table is different from making a table-version, although the table can be itself made, by making a table-version. The notion that all things are version dependent I have already criticized.

Now, returning to plurealism, recall that it differs both from Peirce's view and from Goodman's view, unlike the former in rejecting monism, and unlike the latter in rejecting irrealism, acknowledging instead a mul-tiplicity of independent worlds, worlds we have not made but rather con-front. To every true version there corresponds a world. That is, to every sufficiently credible version I take to be true, I assign a domain I hold to exist, a world objectually understood, independent of my will and my preferences. The implication is that we do not at any time inhabit one world but rather many, corresponding to the several sufficiently credible, if irreducible versions taken, at a given time, to be true. So long as phonol-ogy and botany are mutually irreducible, then, unless further information is introduced, their two domains need to be acknowledged as denizens of consistent but separate worlds. A practical consequence of such acknowl-edgment is that we proceed with inquiries in both domains, taking each, as currently understood, to provide a platform upon which to build further.

This case is not likely to be controversial, but others have been subjects of considerable controversy. The topic of methodological individualism, for example, has occasioned much dialectical argument over whether social science can be reduced to psychology or not, and encouraged the substitu-tion of such argument for substantive inquiries in either psychology or the social sciences themselves. It has further on occasion been assumed that if social sciences could be shown by dialectical argument to be reducible to psychology, short of providing an actual reduction, all inquiry efforts should henceforth be concentrated on furthering the prospects of such reduction. This seems to me clearly a faulty conclusion, for aside from efforts at reduction, there may well be valuable inquiries to be undertaken entirely within the domain of the relevant sciences themselves.

An analogous example relates to the prospect of reducing linguistics to neurology, or to behavioral psychology, or even physics. We have distinguished genuine reduction from mere ontological reduction and cautioned against taking the latter as increasing the likelihood of the genuine variety. Even if we assume the domain of linguistics to refer exclusively to physical entities, such as sounds, morphemes, written characters, organs of speech, etc., the idea that this assumption alone enhances the reduction of linguistics to physics is beyond belief. Even those convinced of the ultimate reduction of linguistics to behavioral psychology or to neurology or physics would need to acknowledge the enormous distance between mere ontological reduction and the genuine variety.

To concentrate all current inquiry on attempts to connect the domain of linguistics to the domain of behavioral psychology or to that of neurology or to that of physics via reduction is certainly premature at present, and in any case presupposes deciding not only on the entities within the relevant domains but also on the propositional content to be assigned the relevant sciences in question. A notable caution of this sort by Chomsky long ago warned that considerable research in linguistics itself would be required, to determine its content, before even considering the prospect of reducing linguistics to any other science.

Although reduction is certainly a worthwhile goal and, where genuine, a source of significant scientific progress, it is not by any means the sole source of progress. For reduction itself depends on the availability of extant sciences eligible for reduction, and these sciences at any given time did not just pop into existence. They have histories and rationales accounting for their formation. They were not always there and there is no reason to suppose they will always be there. The present array of scientific domains is not fixed and there will assuredly be new domains in time if scientific history is any guide. The same processes responsible for the extant array may reasonably be expected to operate similarly in the future. Central to these scientific processes are our motivations, judgments, and purposes, and they are not limited to the aim of reduction. Were reduction alone the sole aim of scientific work, science would consist of a fixed array of domains, to be further reduced, with no additions to be anticipated.

There are, however, as we have earlier intimated, in fact two moments to be acknowledged in making sense of scientific development. One is the reductive moment, the other is the expansive moment. The first is the impulse to simplify, systematize, and contract; the second is the urge to explore, discover, and proliferate. When Quine compared his philosophical taste to his appreciation of desert landscapes, he was expressing his sympathy for the first.[33] When Peirce wrote of the need for science to reject determinism in order to account for evolution's irreversible development of new forms in riotous profusion, he provided a metaphor for the second.[34] Science in fact requires both moments, the one systematizing prevailing clusters of beliefs, the other venturing beyond these clusters in the effort to add to their number. Without the first, science would be simply a collection of uncoordinated propositions; without the second, it would be a stunted, even if to a degree systematized, collection, its capacity for growth frozen in time.

It is perhaps no accident that physicists are drawn more to the reductive moment, trained as they are in mathematical modes of analysis, while biologists are attracted more to the expansive style. Be that as it may, physicists have exalted the ideal of reduction and applauded its achievement whenever it has been accomplished or even approximated, as in the notable case of the reduction of thermodynamics to statistical mechanics, discussed earlier. The increasing success of physical conceptions in bringing wider and wider ranges of credible propositions under its sway has understandably fanned the hope of an ultimate reduction of all such propositions to a single compact physical basis.

As expressing the laudable scientific ideal of systematization, such hope is unobjectionable, as is the related methodological resolve to seek reduction wherever possible. But to assert that a total physicalistic reduction is already guaranteed on dialectical grounds is surely ungrounded. What Goodman has termed "monopolistic physicalism" is no more assured than what might be dubbed "monopolistic phenomenalism, or mentalism." Actual reductions are always desirable, even if piecemeal, but they cannot be established by abstract or dialectical argument alone.

7. A Theory of Everything

Recently, the phrase "a theory of everything" has gained popular currency, but it has been powered by the bold claim that new physical developments have in fact brought such a theory at least within hailing distance. We have earlier noted the complaint of the critics that string theory, the most popular candidate in this connection, has so far yielded no experimental consequences that would make it amenable to empirical test. Yet the notion of a theory of everything has been bolstered as a practical scientific ideal either already achieved or on the verge of being achieved in the relatively near future.

I have already criticized the unqualified notion of a theory of everything. But the idea has a relatively plausible interpretation, for which "everything" refers only to the four forces currently supposed by physicists to account for all physical phenomena, the oustanding and as yet unsolved problem being how to unify all four, including the last, so far resistant to the sought unification. This localized interpretation sets forth a goal for research and speculation in partially familiar conceptual territory which has over several centuries yielded acknowledged results and has come in the recent past tantalizingly close to the desired solution.

To expand the notion to include in fact everything is to outline a task so amorphous and so unlimited as to forfeit any right to be called a task at all. Consider, for example, reducing biology or economics to physics, or neurology, or linguistics, or anthropology, or psychiatry, or theories of literature or of music, or of politics. The list is virtually endless and open-ended, continuing to increase independently of whatever actual reductions may meanwhile have been accomplished.

I have indicated my preference for a plurealistic view, which denies that realism implies monism, thus rejecting a total reduction of all credible systems that I recognize to a single base, while affirming that these systems severally reveal things independent of us. In this latter affirmation, I am, like Peirce, a realist, while, in my pluralism, I share William James' horror of what he called a "block universe," and Goodman's insistence on the existence of satisfactory systems couched in incompatible conceptual terms. My pluralism commits me to acknowledging the existence of indefinitely many worlds, corresponding to the several ontologies presupposed by all unreduced credible systems—neither one world alone, as with monism, nor no worlds at all, as with irrealists or extreme relativists.

Reduction is, of course, a permanent desideratum of science, striving always to systematize, economize, and simplify. But, as I have emphasized earlier, it cannot be achieved on the cheap, via shortcut dialectical argument, without providing the solid proof in any specific case that the conditions of genuine reduction have been met. Short of such proofs, we have, in fact, mere speculation supplementing the actual array of unreduced scientific systems. As explicit reductions are accomplished, serving to reduce this array, science meanwhile continues to develop freely, casting up new concepts and theoretical systems that expand the array, the creativity of the scientific imagination having no limits and no foreseeable end.

In a wide-ranging review of some books on string theory, Freeman Dyson has expressed certain attitudes clearly consistent with pluralist positions as I have outlined them.[35] For one thing, he is not horrified by the specter of two separate worlds, one world describable in classical mechanical terms, the other a subatomic world describable in quantum-mechanical terms. Such equanimity in the face of non-unification is anathema to many contemporary physicists driven, as they are, by the vision of all knowledge ultimately reduced to a unified physics. Pluralism, as already emphasized, rejects such monism in principle, hospitable as it is to variant unreduced systems of any domain.

Second, Dyson forcefully rejects the idea that we will soon "know it all," the reduction of all other sciences to a single physics being assumed as a foregone conclusion by theorists of everything. Third, he takes science as comprehending two enterprises, one he calls "analytic science," the other "synthetic science." This pair is clearly reminiscent of the two moments I distinguished as "the reductive" and the "expansive" within science, the first concentrated on contraction, the second on expansion. Finally, he sums up his attitude by declaring that "science is inexhaustible" and will always remain open. Unlike the so-called "monopolistic physicalism" decried by Goodman, Dyson and pluralists concur in viewing physics at best as an exemplary science, rather than supposing all of science to be, in principle, physics.

I have already noted that pluralism acknowledges several actual worlds rather than just the one. Insofar as we recognize a given theoretical system as sufficiently credible at present for us to assert, provisionally, we are for now committed to its truth. Similarly, we are bound to accept every ontology assumed by theories to the truth of which we are at present committed. We may speculate about the likelihood of future reductions or argue dialectically that such reductions are bound to occur, making it possible to treat reduced systems as mere paraphrases of their reducing counterparts. But so long as such reductions have not already been demonstrated, we are committed to asserting the credible unreduced systems that we now have.

This means that the reduction of the social sciences to a proposed system of methodological individualism, for example, since as yet unrealized, does not release us from our obligation to acknowledge the ontologies of *credible* unreduced social sciences. We need thus to affirm the existence of credible systems, consisting of banking institutions, political states, nations, tribes, etc., yet simultaneously resolving to achieve one or another relevant reduction.

8. The Status of Ethics

A particularly controversial issue concerns the status of ethics. Are ethical assumptions to be accorded similar treatment? To simplify this question, let us take an ethical assumption (or equivalently, value judgment) to be recognizable by its essential incorporation of at least one of a finite list of ethical terms, e.g., "good," bad," "right," "wrong," "ought," or any other definable on the basis of these. Thus, for example, "duty" is an ethical term because it is definable as a task that ought to be performed. (Be it noted that the list of ethical terms in general use, so understood, is finite but indefinitely large.) Ethical assumptions, understood in this way, are, grammatically, indicative statements, presumptively treated as true or false, to be affirmed or denied.

However, as noted in our earlier discussion of theoretical terms in science, the grammatical status of sentences is not decisive in taking them to be truth vehicles, subject to affirmation or denial. Thus, minimal instrumentalists have treated sentences with theoretical terms not as statements functioning as truth vehicles but rather as syntactic linkages connecting genuine statements to others. Similarly, the treatment of ethical assumptions needs to be decided before considering the question of reduction of ethics to science.

9. Emotive Theories; Ayer and Stevenson

Here the issue is, however, not whether ethical assumptions are to be construed as syntactic instruments, but rather whether the terms they contain independently bar them from being truth candidates, without suggesting that they must therefore be syntactical instruments. Extreme emotive theorists, such as A. J. Ayer,[36] interpret ethical sentences as making no assertions, but only evincing feelings of one sort or another, e.g. pleasure or displeasure, anger, disgust, pain, sorrow. To say that a given action was wrong is to refer to the action and then, making no predication, to utter the sound "wrong," a cognate of "Bah" or "Humbug," or an expression of similar emotive—but no cognitive—meaning. To say that the judge's ruling was disgusting is to indicate the ruling in question and then to utter "ugh," or to grunt; to descibe a meal as good is no more an assertion than an approving burp would be.

In any of these cases, truth is obviously irrelevant. The grammatically predicative utterances or sounds in question are of course informative of the respective authors' feelings or states of mind but they do not characterize them; they express them. Nor do they describe their ostensible referents. That the burp or yawn produced by a given person expresses a particular feeling of his is, of course, true or not, a question admitting of evidence. But neither the burp or the yawn is itself predicative, completing an assertion of which it makes sense to ask for the evidence for its truth as distinct from the evidence for its occurrence.

A more moderate emotivist position takes ethical sentences to be hybrids, each composed of at least one genuine statement and one sentence that is no assertion but an emotive expression, evincing the utterer's feelings or efforts to persuade the hearer. The best known position of this sort is that of C. L. Stevenson, whose book *Ethics and Language* presents a ramified discussion of his theory, epitomized by his treatment of the sentence form, "X is good," as composed of two parts, the first stating "I approve of X," and the second saying "Do so as well!"[37]

Clearly, since the imperative component is not an assertion, neither is the compound, and this treatment is extended by Stevenson to all ethical statements. It follows that ethics, acording to the hybrid emotivism we have considered, is not reducible to science at all because of its ineluctable imperative component. The initial components of the diverse ethical sentences we encounter are indeed assertive, but they do not cluster together under presumptive general laws, theories, or generalizations that might be amenable to reduction as such. In sum, neither in toto nor in part, is ethics reducible to science according to the hybrid theory we have considered. Nor, unlike the social theories earlier cited as not reduced to methodological individualism, are we committed to acknowledging the ontologies of the scattered initial assertions of hybrid ethical sentences. For they do not fall under common theories or generalizations, being in each case indexical, the term "I" referring in each sentence solely to its author, and the whole initial assertion of the hybrid bearing not at all on ethics.

10. Moore's Ethical Intuitionism

Aside from emotive theories, there are also intuitionist theories, which exclude reduction of ethics to science for quite independent reasons. The classical modern version of intuitionism is that of G. E. Moore's *Principia Ethica*.[38] Moore argues that ethical terms such as "good" cannot be defined since they are not analyzable as complexes of simples, whereas definability for him requires such analyzability. It follows that no reduction of ethical assumptions containing the term "good" is possible, for such reduction would require "good" to be defined in terms of the reducing science—no science itself containing the term "good."

Nevertheless, ethical assumptions are, for Moore, genuine assertions, true or false. To predicate "good" of a certain entity is to claim that the entity in question possesses a certain simple quality, denoted by the term "good," and perceivable by those who are ethically normal rather than ethically blind. Moore compares "good" in these respects to the term "yellow," which denotes a simple quality and is therefore indefinable, yet is attributable truly or falsely to given surfaces and is perceivable as such by those with normal color vision, but not by the color blind. There may, of course, be disagreements in particular cases as to the applicability of "good," just as there may be such disagreements over "yellow," but one of the claims in each such dispute is true, the other false; there is no basis for concluding that the issue is merely relative, or that at bottom there is only an emotional conflict.

The upshot is, then, that Moore's intuitionism rules out the reducibility of ethics to science, just as emotivism does. Yet there is an important difference between these two treatments of ethics. For emotive theories, whether extreme or moderate, do not consider ethical sentences to be assertions, hence true or false, while Moore's intuitionism insists that they are indeed assertions, either true or false.

Furthermore, Moore, unlike various theological or metaphysical intuitionists, takes the truth or falsity of such assertions to be perceptible to the normal person free of ethical blindness. Hence ethical assertions are for him empirically based judgments, testable through observation, by the exercise of normal perceptive powers. In this respect, ethics is like the sciences, capable of grounding descriptions of particular cases as well as generalizations and theories, by wielding its peculiarly ethical lexicon; indeed, it may be thought of as an autonomous science, irreducible to its sister sciences. In contrast with some other intuitionisms, Moore has a straightforward answer to the natural question: "How can you test attributions of ethical terms in particular cases?" He provides what Quine has called an empirical "checkpoint" which may or may not confirm the truth of the attribution in question by exercising one's normal perception. Is the conclusion, then, that we are indeed committed to the ontology of ethics under Moore's interpretation, as well as to credible assertions as to the distribution of good throughout the world?

This depends, obviously, on who *we* are taken to be. For most of us, I venture to say, the answer is negative; we do not perceive the simple indefinable quality that Moore claimed to perceive. It cannot thus serve for us as an empirical checkpoint in the testing of ethical statements. Further, it seems inconceivable upon reflection that complex ethical problems could be resolved by perception alone—by looking hard in search of a simple quality in the welter of circumstances comprising a serious moral case. Such cases typically involve not just perception but also deliberation, a weighing of conflicting interests and rival motivations issuing in new patterns of conduct and belief rather than the spotting of a pertinent qualitative simple. Finally, Moore's interpretation assumes, without explaining, what Stevenson called the "magnetism" of moral language, the connection between environmental qualities perceived and inclinations enacted, tending to move its hearers in favored directions.

Such magnetism is built into emotive theories from the start by their acknowledging of an imperative component in the normal use of ethical language. But Moore's interpretation gives it no place at all, ignoring the role of ethical language in expressing one's active inclinations and tending to move others as well. To sum up, those who, despite the skeptical considerations mentioned, can accept Moore's interpretation, are indeed committed to acknowledging the ontology of his ethics and its credible assertions though not reducible to science. Those who cannot accept his interpretation need to find other ways to understand ethical language.[39]

11. Dewey and Ethical Naturalism

Some thinkers have insisted that ethical statements are indeed reducible to extant scientific ones. Rather than producing a genuine reduction of ethical assertions to those of an available science, however, they have argued dialectically that ethical terms are definable in scientific terms, and that ethical statements amount to scientific claims. Foremost among such modern thinkers is John Dewey, whose aim is to rebut both intuitionism and relativism as dogmatic approaches to ethics. Only a scientific interpretation, in his view, allows ethical beliefs to be tested by confrontation with empirical evidence and improved accordingly thereby. On what, however, does Dewey base his interpretation?[40]

In various passages of his writings, he says that ethical statements are tantamount to empirical claims concerning the conditions and consequences of the actions under consideration. Recalling Hume's caveat against trying to derive an "ought" from an "is," we puzzle over Dewey's impossible strategy here: How can any descriptive account of an action's conditions or consequences authorize the inference that the action ought (or ought not) to be done? A conjecture I find plausible is this: Dewey supposes ethical problems to arise always in a problem situation, including not only the subject's factual beliefs but also his inclinations, sets, and preferences, his problem being to decide what course of action ought to be chosen. These inclinations, sets, and preferences are expressible as ethical statements held by him, serving as tacit premises in the derivation of "ought" conclusions.[41]

Dewey calls his interpretation naturalistic but does not construe it as requiring reduction in the genuine scientific sense I have referred to heretofore. He does not express his ethical views as a general theory but as a mode of understanding the diverse ethical assertions people make in response to their several problem situations. These assertions are for him naturalistic in not invoking supernaturalistic agencies, in constituting genuine statements, and in susceptibility to scientific methods of empirical testing and evidence. But reducibility after the manner of thermodynamics' reduction to statistical mechanics is not in his purview. He wants, above all, to shun occult forces, dogmatic intuitions, and the sharp sundering of ethics from science and common practice. But in so construing ethical statements, Dewey relativizes them to the particular problem situation of the agent, inclusive of the agent's sets, preferences, and various inclinations. It does not follow that the agent's understanding of his problem situation must be fixed and held dogmatically come what may. Indeed, Dewey rejects the idea of fixed ends, as well as the notion that no dispute is possible over ends, emphasizing the continuity of ends and means as well as the mutual interactions of facts and desires within the relevant historical setting. Science, in his view, in helping to reveal the likely continuities and interactions to be expected, clarifies the agent's view of his problems and opens his eyes to their structures and potentials.

The possibility of there eventually arising a general theory of ethics of course remains, and there are even now proffered definitions of ethical terms, serving as enthymemes bridging the Humean chasm between "is" and "ought." Utilitarian and deontological varieties in this genre abound, but neither in specificity nor in common acceptance does any such definition approximate a general theory in the scientific sense. The present state of analytic discussions of ethics is still, I conclude, far from achieving consensus in theory, or with specific reference to reduction.

I have earlier insisted that the reductive moment in the history of science is far from exclusive, there being also an expansive moment, more akin to biological than to physical turns of mind, and in which proliferation is the focus rather than economy. It is important to recognize that, aside from reduction, we may encourage exploration in the interest of expansion, and that as yet unachieved reduction is not a failure, much less a crisis, but an opportunity. This opportunity is actually twofold: to add new realms to the old, and to investigate the relations between such new realms and old, as well as those holding between any realm and any other. The failure to reduce one to the other does not impede efforts to relate them, whether by projected definitions of significant terms, or by inquiring into other sorts of connection obtaining between them.

Certainly, efforts to relate one scientific cluster to another may stimulate eventual progress toward a genuine reduction. But there are outstanding examples of important commonalities across clusters made visible through attention to their relations, though leading to no reduction. Pragmatic thinkers have been especially noted for their comprehensive attention to a variety of human enterprises and their articulation of unifying commonalities linking them. Thus, Dewey refined his notion of problem solving out of his inquiries into the psychology of thinking, characterizing child development as well as the work of the laboratory, his conception of experience as relating the experimental work of the scientist to the inventive creativity of the artist. His predecessor Peirce pioneered his theory of signs, or semei-otic, outlining what he took to be underlying affinities among sign functions in language, in gesture, in expression, in pictorial and graphical representation, etc., culminating in an analysis of dimensions of significa-tion, with applications to diverse initiatives, such as science, mathematics, cartography, drama, medicine, literature, pictorial and musical arts, among others.

A more recent example is the pragmatically inclined work of Nelson Goodman, whose *Languages of Art* associates the arts and the sciences, rejecting the time-worn division between the two, the former as presum-ably emotive, the latter as cognitive.[42] Goodman's tendency to override traditional divisions in search of sigificant commonalities is reminiscent of Dewey. It appears again in the above work in his masterly "theory of symbols," which employs ramified notions of denotation, expression, and exemplification to explain recurrent forms of semantic function in the sci-ences and in disparate arts, inclusive of literature, drama, painting, music, architecture, and dance.

12. Symbol, Reference, and Ritual

Goodman's work challenges self-imposed philosophical restrictions to the scientific and the formal, thus returning to a more generous prag-matic view and opening the way to new investigations in all areas of symbolism.

In this spirit, the discussion that follows turns from the arts to ritual, drawing on studies reported in my book, *Inquiries*, that outline multiple symbolic functions of rites.[43] Such functions include denotation, exempli-fication, and reenactment, all of which serve, in religious, cultural, and institutional contexts, to mark out structures of historical time, space, and community. In addition, patterns of ritual repetition bring performers' minds into regular contact with symbolized properties, thus influencing their concepts and sensibilities.

The focus on symbolic aspects is an act of abstraction. It must not be taken as denying the importance of the social and institutional func-tions of ritual, nor of the belief system which, in every case, provides its context and motivation. On the other hand, to abstract from such features in order to concentrate on the symbolism of rites draws special attention to their cognitive roles, that is, their roles in conceptualization and reference and, consequently, in shaping the mental sensibilities and habits of their participants, whether independently judged favorably or not.

The mere assignment of cognitive roles to ritual comes into conflict with its frequent devaluation as a hindrance to spontaneous religious feeling. Thus, William James' *Varieties of Religious Experience* begins by dividing the religious domain into the institutional and the personal, proceeding thereafter "to ignore the institutional branch entirely." The sort of religion in which James is himself interested gives rise, as he says, to "personal not ritual acts, the individual transacts the business by himself alone, and the ecclesiastical organization, with its priests and sacraments and other go-betweens, sinks to an altogether secondary place. The relation goes direct from heart to heart, from soul to soul between man and his maker." Assimilated by James to institutional machinery that slows or obstructs the free flow of religious sentiment, ritual is here mentioned only to be dismissed.

It is true that, where it has not been thus dismissed, ritual has been assigned not to feeling but to the contrasting realm of cognition—but with equally devaluing effects. For it has here been associated with myth, which is viewed as defective cognition, bad science, pathological belief. Whether a hindrance to religious emotion or an objectification of falsehood or illusion, ritual has not often been considered as serving properly cognitive functions.

Two recent thinkers may be considered as pioneers of the symbolic treatment I offer: Ernst Cassirer and Susanne Langer. Cassirer proposes to redress the devaluative attitudes just described, interpreting mythical thought, always associated with ritual, as a positive stage in the development of science. Resting on a unity of feeling that views nature as "one great society, *the society of life*," myth perceives *physiognomic* rather than objective features—structuring a "dramatic world—a world of actions, of forces, of conflicting powers. . . . Mythical perception is always impregnated with these emotional qualities." This world is the first stage in the development of human thought, in turn overcome by the "world of our sense perceptions," which is, in its turn, succeeded by the generalizing concepts peculiar to the scientific understanding of the physical world. None of Cassirer's three stages is "a mere illusion," science does not "extirpate [its predecessors] root and branch," although it must abstract from them in order to attain the objectivity required for its own function.

Although Cassirer does indeed deny that myth constitutes "a mere mass of unorganized and confused ideas," and affirms its role in structuring a world from which our "empirical thought" has grown, he sees its virtue to lie not in its own cognitive deliverances but in its giving way developmentally to an eventually maturing science. His defense of myth and ritual is limited by its underlying contrast of emotion and science, strengthening the dubious view that cognition is scientific or nothing and the equally dubious view that scientific cognition is devoid of emotion.

Langer, unlike Cassirer, separates ritual from myth, associating myth with fantasy and dream but relating ritual rather to religious feeling, which is "bound . . . to set occasions, when the god-symbol is brought forth and officially contemplated." At first, "an unconscious issue of feelings into shouting and prancing," the agitation evolves into "a habitual reaction . . . used to *demonstrate*, rather than to relieve, the feelings of individuals." The overt act has in this phase become a gesture—no longer a symptom of feeling but a symbol of it—denoting it and thus bringing it to mind. As an articulation of feelings, ritual produces "not a simple emotion but a complex permanent attitude . . . an emotional pattern, which governs all individual lives. . . . A rite regularly performed is the constant reiteration of sentiments toward 'first and last things'; it is not a free expression of emotions, but a disciplined rehearsal of 'right attitudes.'"

Langer, more clearly than Cassirer, separates the display of feelings from their articulation. As gestures, rituals are for her primarily symbolic or referential, denoting rather than evincing feeling. The feelings they denote record "man's response [to] the basic facts of human existence" as expressed by the sacred life-symbol arising in myth. But, regularly repeated, the ritual reference to such responses in itself shapes attitudes and forms habitual dispositions.

Langer is certainly right, I believe, in emphasizing the formalization of ritual and its gestural, that is, its symbolic character. But her interpretation is too restricted both in its conception of the symbolic process itself and in its designation of the objects symbolized in ritual. For she thinks of the process as *denotation* strictly, and she conceives the objects to be uniformly *feelings*. Rituals may, however, symbolize anything, not just feelings; as Cassirer put it, "a dramatic world—a world of actions, of forces, of conflicting powers." And the process of symbolization need not be restricted to denotation but may encompass other forms of reference as well. Indeed, ritual is typically symbolic in several modes simultaneously, and gathers strength thereby. The oft-noted capacity of ritual to survive changes in doctrinal interpretation may stem just from being linked by diverse bonds of reference to objects. When one or more are cut, the others hold fast. In the remainder of this discussion, I extend the symbolic interpretation of Cassirer and Langer, without relying on the division betweeen emotion and cognition. In contrast to both these authors, I emphasize the varieties of symbolic function displayed by rituals, and require neither special emotive qualities nor peculiar emotive objects.

We have seen that Langer speaks of ritual acts as *denoting*, thus regarding denotation as going beyond mere verbal description. Goodman not only endorses this broadening of the notion, understanding it to comprehend pictorial, gestural, and other sorts of representation. In addition, he expands the idea of *reference*, so that it encompasses not merely denotation but also *exemplification* and *expression*. We shall see that rituals may, accordingly, be understood as engaged in exemplifying and expressing, in addition to denoting. But how are these two new functions themselves to be interpreted?

To begin with, exemplification is the relation *being a sample of*: it relates a thing to those of its properties to which it also refers. A tailor's swatch, as Goodman explains, "does not exemplify all its properties; it is a sample of color, weave, texture, and pattern, but not of size, shape, or absolute weight or value." Expression he treats as implying metaphorical exemplification, that is, reference by an object to a property it metaphorically possesses. Thus a given painting may, at one and the same time, denote a man, literally exemplify certain hues or patterns, and express—that is, metaphorically exemplify—melancholy.

Not only words and pictures but also gestures may denote, exemplify, and express. Ritual gestures, in particular, may denote or represent historical events, or events thought to be historical; they may portray expected occurrences or hoped-for outcomes, they may denote or purport to denote persons, gods, or things. They may perform this role through bodily movement, after the manner of mime; they may also employ the voice in song or speech. The range of ritual gestures indeed comprehends verbal gestures; thus, any denotative role that can be fulfilled by verbal means is also within the scope of ritual reference. Objects employed in ritual may also stand for, or refer, in a wide variety of ways.

Although not every ritual gesture denotes, every such gesture typically has specifications or prescriptions that it must satisfy. These may be transmitted orally or written down or understood in context, but that there is a right and a wrong way of execution is normally evident. It is this fact that constitutes the formalization of ritual gestures emphasized by Langer, who describes them as "bound to an often meticulously exact repetition, which gradually makes their forms as familiar as words or tunes." What Cassirer says of sacrificial services may be considerably generalized: "The . . . service is fixed by very definite objective rules, a set sequence of words and acts which must be carefully observed if the sacrifice is not to fail in its purpose." Now a proper performance of a rite often functions as a sample of it, that is, it literally exemplifies it. In this way, it lends itself to auxiliary use as a demonstration in the process of teaching the rite to learners. Rituals may thus be passed on, through participation which both satisfies their normative requirements and educates people in their use.

We have seen that Goodman treats expression as implying metaphorical exemplification. A picture may exemplify not only a certain style or pattern but also a certain feeling or movement, possessing the style or pattern literally, the feeling or movement metaphorically, but in both cases constituting a sample of, and referring to, the property possessed. A rite expressing a certain feature may, analogously, be taken as metaphorically possessing it and also referring to it. Particular rituals may thus be interpreted as expressing a wide range of features—for example, joy or sorrow, triumph or grief, elation or trust, yearning, contrition, or exaltation. The multiply symbolic character of ritual should here be recalled. Whatever a given rite may in fact denote, it may simultaneously exemplify, literally or metaphorically, quite different things. Explicitly representing episodes of a sacred story, it may at the same time express, rather than represent, dependence or victory, atonement or thirst for redemption.

The symbol expressing a feature must possess it. Must the user or producer or viewer of the symbol also possess it? Not so. "The properties a symbol expresses are its own property," writes Goodman. "That the actor was despondent, the artist high, the spectator gloomy or nostalgic or euphoric, the subject inanimate, does not determine whether the face or picture is sad or not. The cheering face of the hypocrite expresses solicitude, and the stolid painter's picture of boulders may express agitation." Similarly, the feelings, thoughts, or other mental states of performers or spectators of a rite are to be distinguished from the features expressed by the rite itself.

Yet we here confront a striking contrast between arts and rites, ritual presenting a radically different aspect. For rituals are, in religious as distinct from magical contexts, typically intended to penetrate to the heart. Performers of rites are not actors. The question, "Does he truly believe what he is saying?" is relevant to the ritual performer alone, while artful simulation of belief is a feat valued only in the actor. Although both actors and performers of religious ritual may indeed perform flawlessly while their thoughts and feelings are remote from the features expressed, a major point of ritual, although not of drama, is to affect the thoughts and feelings of participants, in part through repeated exposure to such features. We have seen Langer's emphasis on ritual repetition. Unlike a dramatic performance, a religious ritual usually has a characteristic pattern of recurrence; it is to be repeated with the seasons, or with other units of time, or with the important junctures of a life. Such regular recurrence functions to pattern the sensibilities of participants, in good part by repeated contact with features denoted, literally exemplified, or expressed.

True, not every expressed feature is, even theoretically, to be paralleled in the participant, in ritual as in art. For example, a rite expressing majesty may rather be hoped to induce faith or trust. And even where parallel features are indeed hoped for, successful execution of a rite on any given occasion does not hinge on satisfaction of this hope; that a participant's state of mind is incongruous with the expressed theme of the rite may lower its quality but does not, in general, argue that the rite has not taken place. Yet quality may indeed be affected, and this is a significant point: there is, in the case of ritual, a certain expected linkage between expressed properties and participants' mentality and sensibility; the cognition of expressed features, reinforced by repeated performance, is a major medium of such linkage. Regular recurrence is not only, as suggested by Cassirer and Langer, a force for the stylization of ritual acts; it is a way of strengthening their influence on the mind.

The ideal ritual participant is one whose own character is suitably affected by the role he performs and not simply one who skillfully conveys the character defined by his role. Although in drama the cheering face of the hypocrite may, as Goodman says, express solicitude, hypocrisy being irrelevant, it is absurd to suppose that hypocrisy is irrelevant to performance of a religious rite expressive, say, of contrition or repentance. Although in both cases hypocrisy is independent of what is expressed by the performance, it is only in the ritual case relevant to understanding the whole pattern of associated performances, functioning as it does to reduce hypocrisy in the participants themselves.

I have emphasized the importance of ritual recurrence in forcefully calling to mind those properties the rite denotes, exemplifies, or expresses. But this is not the whole story, for rituals, as R. S. Peters has remarked, "help to unite the past with the future and to convey the sense of participation in a shared form of life."[44] They comprise not merely repeated action patterns but traditions, conveying, beyond each repetition of a performance, some sense of the fact that it *is* a repetition, some awareness of its predecessors. And such awareness I interpret in terms of an additional mode of symbolization that I call "reenactment."

I reserve the notion of *reenactment* for the relation between a ritual performance and its preceding ritual replicas, rather than using it, as is sometimes customary, for the relation between a performance and the event it commemorates. "Reenactment," in my usage, is a reproduction of the act, a co-exemplification of the same rite. Commemorated events, on the other hand, are typically denoted, represented, or portrayed rather than reproduced in ritual, even though the ritual aim may be to promote spiritual union with the historical agents in question. Even mimetic gestures do not, in general, reproduce the mimed activity; they exemplify some of its features, but not the activity itself, although they many vividly call it to mind. On the other hand, a performance that replicates earlier performances of a given rite reproduces them in constituting a sample of— or exemplifying—the selfsame rite.

In thus reproducing its earlier ritual replicas, each ritual performance refers indirectly to them, alludes to them, that is, while independently denoting whatever it may denote, and symbolizing in the other modes so far distinguished. In the regular recurrence of a rite, a sense thus builds up, in each new performance, of the prior performances to which it is ritually kin. The performance thus calls to mind not only the event that may be commemorated, but also the sequence of vehicles of its commemoration.

The relation of one performance to a replica is a relation holding between performances denoted by, and exemplifying, the same ritual specifications. The allusion by a present performance to earlier replicas may be thought of as transmitted through a two-link chain of exemplification as follows: the present performance is linked to the ritual specification it exemplifies, and this specification is in turn linked to past performances exemplifying it.

It is worth noting that such chains, widely available, become referentially operative only in certain cases. Thus, reenactment plays virtually no role in the arts, by comparison with religious ritual. A given performance of a musical work typically makes no reference to the past performances of the same work, although it may single out special performances as landmarks for comparison. By contrast, a ritual performance alludes to its own past kin, fostering in participants a sense of reenacting an important procedure. The relevant chain is referentially activated, and such activation is one symptom of the religious consciousness.

The marking out of ritually commemorated events helps to define a temporal matrix, and reenactment elaborates it further by articulating an ever-expanding ritual tradition. Concomitantly, reenactment serves also to form a conception of community. For the performers of past ritual replicas consitute a body of actors to which present performers relate themselves through reenactment and, hence, indirectly to one another. The community thus defined bears not only common bonds to the past but also common orientations in the present and outlooks for the future. Thus, an organization of time, as well as of the space occupied by a historical comminity, is facilitated.

This is perhaps the root of the emphasis on stabilization in primitive religion, in the work of Bergson, Cassirer, and others. In this vein Cassirer writes, agreeing with Bergson, "primitive religion can ... leave no room for any freedom of individual thought. It prescribes its fixed, rigid, inviolable rules not only for every human action but also for every human feeling." But as I have pictured it, the general phenomenon of ritual is no mere squelching of emotion, no cage of the feelings. Rather we have to do with a cognitive ordering of categories of time, space, action, and community. Nor is ritual peculiar to religious institutions, characterizing a wide variety of social, cultural, and political functions that engender a sense of tradition and community. Speaking of the rituals of Parliament, R. S. Peters writes, "Such rituals help to unite the past with the future and to convey the sense of participation in a shared form of life. They do much, too, to develop that feeling of fraternity which is the life-blood of any effective institution."[45]

Returning to our earlier discussion of scientific clusters, it is worth repeating that, independently of reduction, and aside from the formulation of important affinities between such clusters, the mere identification of a new such cluster satisfies the scientific impulse to explore new ground, giving rein to curiosity for its own sake. In encouraging such curiosity in every quarter, philosophy is at one with science, with art, and with every adventure of the free human mind.

Notes

1   W. V. Quine, *Philosophy of Logic* (Englewood Cliffs, NJ: Prentice-Hall, 1970), p. 12.

2   O. Neurath, "Protocol Sentences," and M. Schlick, "The Foundation of Knowledge," both reprinted in *Logical Positivism*, A. J. Ayer, ed. (New York: Free Press, 1959), 199ff and 209ff. For discussion, see also Scheffler, *Science of Subjectivity* (Indianapolis: Hackett, 1985), ch. 5.

3   C. S. Peirce, *Collected Papers of Charles Sanders Peirce*, Charles Hartshorne and Paul Weiss, eds. (Cambridge, MA: Harvard University Press, 1934), 6.485. See also Scheffler, *Four Pragmatists: A Critical Introduction to Peirce, James, Mead and Dewey* (London: Routledge & Kegan Paul, 1974), p. 113.

4   Peirce, *Collected Papers*, 1.8–14 and 1.171.

5   Peirce, *Collected Papers*, 5.407.

6   Scheffler, ibid., pp. 79, 100.

7   John Dewey, *Logic: The Theory of Inquiry* [1938] (Carbondale: Southern Illinois University Press, 1986), p. 343, n. 6.

8   Nelson Goodman, *Ways of Worldmaking* (Indianapolis: Hackett, 1978), pp. 123–24.

9   Goodman, ibid., p. 122.

10 Nelson Goodman, *Problems and Projects* (Indianapolis: Bobbs-Merrill, 1972), pp. 233, 236.

11 See W. V. Quine, *From a Logical Point of View* (Cambridge, MA: Harvard University Press, 1961), ch. 7.

12 Goodman, *Ways of Worldmaking*, op. cit., p. 96.

13 See Israel Scheffler, "My Quarrels with Nelson Goodman," *Philosophy and Phenomenological Research* 62, no. 3 (2001): 665–77.

14 Israel Scheffler, *Symbolic Worlds* (Cambridge: Cambridge University Press, 1997), p. 209, n. 27.

15 P. McCormick, ed. *Starmaking* (Cambridge, MA: MIT Press, 1996), p. 166.

16 Ibid., p. 213.

17 Nelson Goodman, *Of Mind and Other Matters* (Cambridge, MA: Harvard University Press, 1984), p. 42.
18 Ibid., p. 41.
19 Goodman, *Ways of Worldmaking*, op. cit., p. x.
20 Israel Scheffler, "Reply to Goodman," in McCormick, op. cit., pp. 162–63.
21 McCormick, ibid., p. 173.
22 Moritz Schlick, "The Foundation of Knowledge" (trans. D. Rynin) in Ayer, *Logical Positivism*, pp. 215, 226.
23 C. I. Lewis, *Mind and the World Order*, op. cit., pp. 191–92.
24 Peirce, *Collected Papers*, 5.384.
25 Ibid., 5.407. This passage appears in Peirce's paper, "How to Make Our Ideas Clear."
26 Peirce, *Collected Papers*, ibid.
27 Ibid., 8.12.
28 W. V. Quine, *Word and Object* (Cambridge, MA: Technology Press of MIT and New York: John Wiley, 1960), p. 23.
29 See Thomas S. Kuhn, *The Structure of Scientific Revolutions* (Chicago and London: University of Chicago Press, 1962), and Scheffler, *Science and Subjectivity*, 2nd ed., op. cit., ch. 4 and appendix A therein.
30 Ibid.
31 See Israel Scheffler, "A Plea for Plurealism," *Transactions of the Peirce Society* 35, no. 3 (1999): 425–36. Much of the following discussion is drawn from this paper.
32 Nelson Goodman, *The Structure of Appearance*, 3rd ed. (Boston: Reidel, 1977), pp. 10, 21–22.
33 Quine, *From a Logical Point of View*, op. cit., p. 4.
34 Peirce, "The Doctrine of Necessity Examined." See esp. *Collected Papers*, 6.14, 6.36, 6.39, and 6.44. Peirce argues that mechanical forces cannot explain diversity but, more important, cannot explain increasing diversity over time, facts of growth or evolution which are irreversible.
35 Freeman Dyson, "The World on a String," *New York Review of Books*, May 13, 2004.
36 A. J. Ayer, *Language, Truth and Logic* (New York: Dover Publications, 1952), pp. 20ff and ch. 6.
37 C. L. Stevenson, *Ethics and Language* (New Haven: Yale University Press, 1944), chs. 2 and 4.
38 G. E. Moore, *Principia Ethica* (Cambridge: Cambridge University Press, 1903).
39 See, e.g., K. Baier, *The Moral Point of View* (Ithaca: Cornell University Press, 1958), William K. Frankena, *Ethics* (Englewood Cliffs, NJ: Prentice Hall, 1963), P. H. Nowell-Smith, *Ethics* (Harmondsworth, Middlesex: Penguin, 1959, 1965).

40 John Dewey, *The Quest for Certainty* (Carbondale: Southern Illinois University Press, 1929), ch. 10.

41 Israel Scheffler, "Israel Scheffler Interviewed by Harvey Siegel," *Journal of Philosophy of Education* 39, no. 4 (2005): 657–59.

42 See Chapter 6.

43 *Inquiries* (Indianapolis: Hackett, 1986), and Chapter 7. My discussion also draws on portions of my "Symbol, Ritual and Cognition," in V. M. Colapietro and T. M. Olshevsky, eds., *Peirce's Doctrine of Signs* (Berlin and New York: Mouton de Gruyter, 1996), pp. 173–180 (largely verbatim).

44 R. S. Peters, *Ethics and Education* (London: George Allen and Unwin, 1966, 1970), pp. 318–19.

45 Ibid.

Part II

Related Pragmatic Themes

Chapter 4

Belief and Method

Introduction

Pragmatism is popularly taken to be simply an attitude or a style, an emphasis on the practical or the social to the detriment of theoretical reflection and individual values.* There are natural causes for such a construal, aside from the mere connotation of the word itself in everyday use. For pragmatic thinkers do in fact lay great stress upon practice, emphasizing the role of action in human thought, from the humblest bit of learning by a child exploring its room, to the most refined learning of the scientist manipulating the environment experimentally in order to explore the universe. Pragmatists, moreover, stress the social import of thinking—the structure of science as a community of investigators, the influence of historical contexts on the course of philosophy, and the relevance of philosophical inquiry to the problems of men.

Nevertheless, the popular conception of pragmatism is extremely misleading, untrue to the movement as a whole and to the works of its individual thinkers. For while it accurately reflects pragmatic emphases on action and society, it neglects to represent such emphases as arising out of philosophical inquiry, failing utterly to register the source of such inquiry in a struggle with abstract questions and issues. Seeing pragmatism simply as an emphasis, it ignores pragmatic efforts to formulate philosophical accounts of meaning and thought, truth and knowledge, reality and value.

---

* I have drawn upon the treatment in my *Four Pragmatists* (London: Routledge & Kegan Paul, 1974), for various aspects of the present chapter, which originally appeared as "Pragmatism as a Philosophy" in K. Oehler, ed., *Zeichen und Realität* (Tübingen: Stauffenburg Verlag, 1984).

No investigation of such efforts can avoid the conclusion that pragmatism is a serious philosophy, with deep roots in the philosophical tradition. With the exception of William James, whose thought derived from British empiricism, the Cambridge pragmatists were indeed, as Murphey has called them, Kant's children,[1] and the movement as a whole may be largely interpreted as an extension of Kantian themes into the scientific and social worlds of the nineteenth century. Charles Sanders Peirce, who took the very name "pragmatism" from Kant, was steeped in the history of philosophy and developed his thinking through interaction with the great philosophical masters of the past as well as the science and mathematics of his own day. Rejecting Cartesianism, he formulated challenging new conceptions of meaning and reality through reflection on the methods of the natural sciences, and strove all his life to develop a complete system of philosophy, in the spirit of the Kantian architectonic.

William James, a sensitive psychologist as well as a bold philosophical thinker, sought not only to advance the empirical study of mental phenomena but also to develop an adequate metaphysical interpretation of such phenomena and of the main features of human life as known to us by whatever source. He sought a view that would, in particular, do justice to individual freedom, to the reality of human choice, and to the stubbornness and disjointedness of particular facts as against what he called the "block universe" of Idealism. George Herbert Mead, philosopher and social psychologist, worked out a developmental approach to the mind–body problem, in which the central role was played by symbolism. Starting from Wilhelm Wundt's theory of gesture as communication of meaning, Mead elaborated a radical view of mind and self, as well as language, as emerging out of society, rather than the reverse. His study of symbolism yielded rich and suggestive interpretations of communication, conscience, and human community. Finally, John Dewey, who began his thinking career as a Hegelian, retained forever after characteristic marks of his Hegelian beginnings: a pronounced developmentalism, a respect for the force of ideas, and, above all, an urge to unify opposites—to achieve a vision of the inclusive whole within which particular doctrines in conflict may be seen to represent but partial accounts of reality.

These pragmatist thinkers were intellectually and spiritually very different. Peirce's inspiration was the logic of science; his vision was of the ideal and the general: the ideal community of investigators, the general purport of ideas, the long-run approximation to reality through the self-corrective method of science. James's inspiration was rather the individual life of the individual creature, the predicaments of personal choice, the open options defining the particular act, the flow of time and mind, the religious perspective of the single human agent. Mead's vision was, further, social and evolutionary, his effort to understand the distinctive features of human community, as made possible through the growth of symbolic function. And Dewey's aim was in the broadest sense practical and moral, to reconstruct human arrangements through fostering the habit of intelligence—making reflection practical and practice reflective by relating both thought and action to their anticipated meanings in experience.

Although different in their several primary concerns and emphases, these pragmatic thinkers nevertheless joined in producing a distinctive philosophical orientation, rooted in the intellectual past but responsive to the intellectual challenges of the present. They sought indeed to bring philosophical conceptions up-to-date through analysis of the new science and its methods, while placing science itself within a philosophical framework featuring a new approach to meaning. And they sought further to apply their philosophical conceptions in understanding the unprecedented circumstances and the challenges facing human society in the modern world.

The nineteenth-century world in which pragmatism developed was a world in which important oppositions were at work: science versus religion, positivism versus romanticism, intuition versus sense experience. The characteristic posture of pragmatism in response to such oppositions was that of a mediating philosophy, attempting to bridge science and religion, theory and practice, fact and value, speculative thought and analysis, tender-minded and tough-minded temperaments (as James put it), and (with Dewey) school and life. This mediating posture differentiates pragmatism from other philosophical tendencies inspired by science. In particular, pragmatism contrasts with positivism in refusing to assimilate intellectual interests generally to some simplified model of positive science. Responsive in particular to evolutionary thought and the new statistical modes of inference, pragmatism was indeed led to revise inherited conceptions of science itself. And, rather than using science as a device for dismissing or downgrading other modes of experience, such as art, history, morality, religion, philosophy, and social practice, pragmatism has taken science primarily as exemplifying general concepts of critical thought, in terms of which important continuities among all the modes might be revealed, and in light of which they might all be refined and brought to bear intelligently upon human problems.

1. Problems of Pragmatism and Pragmatic Responses

Pragmatism developed in a period of enormous social and intellectual change—a time that Max Fisch has named the "classical period" in America, from the end of the Civil War to the eve of the Second World War.[2] Dewey's life spanned this period, and Gail Kennedy has described its course as follows:

> He was born on the eve of the great war that was to ensure the triumph in America of industrialism and economic enterprise, in the year that Darwin published his *Origin of Species*, the book which marked the coming of age of modern science. He grew up in the environment of the older America, in the Vermont town of Burlington. Here life was still largely unaffected by the newer science and by modern industrialism. From this small community with its simple and intimate round of handicraft and agricultural occupations, the form of society that Jefferson knew, he was to go out into the complex world created by modern science and mass-production industries, to the first American university, the newly founded Johns Hopkins, to the fermenting democracy of the Middle West, in his years of teaching at the Universities of Michigan and Minnesota, then to the great industrial and commercial cities of Chicago and New York. Dewey has said in an autobiographical essay that the forces which influenced him came "from persons and from situations" rather than from books. It was the transition from the America of his boyhood to the new America of his maturity that created the basic problems and formed the central theme of his philosophy.[3]

This period of transition brought with it major intellectual, and not merely social, changes. Not only was there a challenge in science to traditional religion and morality; there was also a challenge to inherited conceptions of science and classical views of knowledge. The most important influence was that of evolution, promoting the biologizing of human intelligence and the continuity between mankind's capacities and those of the lower animals. The rise of experimental and historical sciences of man, as well, reinforced evolutionary ideas of process and continuity, and also brought out the adaptive variability in human custom. The new prominence of probabilistic and statistical concepts both in physics and biology required a revision of older conceptions of logic and science. Finally, while great social changes were complicating life, making liberty and choice more precarious, the new human sciences painted a more flexible picture to replace older notions of cultural fixity; the idea of a *social* science indeed held out the prospect of bringing tradition itself under a measure of control. Knowledge, it seemed, had now to be reconceived: arising out of a biological matrix, continuous with adaptive action addressed to environmental problems, it yielded provisional solutions rather than necessary truths, promising increased social control but therefore imposing increased moral responsibility.[4]

The changes here noted were taken by pragmatism to pose the following broad philosophical problems. First, how is our contemporary theory of knowledge to assimilate the new scientific understanding of change, of process, of biological and social factors, of probable reasoning? Classical rationalism and classical empiricism seemed both inadequate to the task, the one taking knowing as the work of the individual mind drawing up eternal truths from within, the other as the mind's passively registering ideas stamped on it from without.

Second, and more generally, how are we to articulate the new emphasis on *continuity*, connecting man's life with the world of nature, relating his knowledge and his values, his cognitions with his feelings and actions, his life as an intellect with his career as an organism in a particular biological and evolutionary setting? The basic problem, for pragmatism, was to find a way of overcoming inherited dualisms of knower and known, mind and body, fact and value, theory and practice, ends and means.

Third, how are we to find new sources of stability in the face of radical changes in scientific belief and—more urgently still—how to find sources of stability consonant with the experimental habit of mind underlying science? Rejecting what Dewey called "the quest for certainty" and adopting instead Peirce's attitude of "fallibilism," how could sufficient stability yet be found to sustain the arts of inquiry, of education, of culture, and the public life?

Fourth, how are we to conceive the prospects of individual selfhood and democratic community under the new conditions of industrial society? How can policy formation be institutionalized in today's circumstances so as to be responsive to those whom policy affects? How can technological advance be reconciled with humane purpose, with the values of the arts and of associated life, and with the primacy of critical intelligence as the chief ideal of education?

The pragmatists' response to these problems cannot be recounted here in any detail, but its main features may be related, in outline, to a single starting point, namely, the rejection of Cartesian philosophy. Rejecting the mind–body dualism of Descartes, pragmatism is, first of all, led to develop a *functional view of thought*, relating cognition to the purposive life of the organism, responding to problems set by its environment. Second, giving up Cartesian certainty, pragmatism proposes instead a *fallibilistic view of knowledge* as a provisional scheme of hypotheses, resting upon probable reasoning and pointed toward the future, remaining ever subject to the test of further experience. Third, surrendering Cartesian individualism, pragmatists offer in its place a *social conception of science* as the effort, not of single inquirers, but of an open-ended community of investigators to learn from experience in a systematic way. Finally, giving up Cartesian intuition, pragmatists alternatively propose the *representative character of thinking*, holding thought to be always and throughout symbolic, channeled through networks of interdependent sign processes, thus incapable of ever yielding either fixity or certainty. Symbolism enables thought to frame ends-in-view independent of actual outcomes, and so to anticipate and regulate conduct. Thus, writes Dewey, "The invention or discovery of symbols is doubtless by far the single greatest event in the history of man." Signs or symbols themselves are not *images or pictures* of reality; they are rather to be interpreted as devices of the purposeful life. "What now is a *conception*?" asks William James, and he answers: "It is a *teleological instrument*. It *is* a partial aspect of a thing which *for our purpose* we regard as its essential aspect, as the representative of the entire thing." "Wherever intelligence operates," writes Dewey, "things are judged in their capacity of signs of other things. If scientific knowledge enables us to estimate more accurately the worth of things as signs, we can afford to exchange a loss of theoretical certitude for a gain in practical judgment. For if we can judge events as indications of other events, we can prepare in all cases for the coming of what is anticipated," and take part as knowers in the purposive "direction of change."[5]

The consequences of these anti-Cartesian positions are far-reaching. Once certainty and individualism are surrendered as epistemic ideals and science reinterpreted as the continuous learning effort of an ideal community, stability is to be sought in the *intellectual method* defining such community. The conclusions of particular inquiries are indeed all provisional; they are probable at best and subject to revision by further investigation. But despite recurrent revisions of scientific doctrine, the community dedicated to systematic learning from experience is itself a continuous entity, unified by its allegiance to critical method. It is such allegiance that gives us ground to stand on even as we alter particular items of belief. The very self-correctiveness of science which forces the revision of its theories when they fall out of accord with the evidence constitutes a steady ideal standing firm throughout change. And while we cannot hope to be sure of any of our particular theories, we can be sure that the method of science will yield increasingly adequate theories through continued inquiry by the investigative community of mankind.

This investigative community offers, finally, a suggestive model for conceiving democratic society generally. As science institutionalizes procedures for investigating hypotheses about nature, so democratic society institutionalizes procedures for the critical testing of social ideas, plans, and policies all to be conceived as hypothetical. Provisional agreements on particulars, whether in scientific research or in social action, are necessary and, indeed, sufficient to organize further collaborative efforts, but all particular ideas remain subject to the continuing test of experience, to be revised when necessary, in accord with the underlying unity of method.

In science, the open communication of ideas and their availability for testing by rival theorists is an essential point of method. In democratic society, too, an essential need is to ensure free communication among persons, so that their special perspectives may be appreciated by others and made available, moreover, for the general testing of social arrangements. Dewey's notion of *shared experience* does not refer to the having of the same experiences by all, but rather to the communication of diverse experiences by means of shared symbolic structures. The social problem is to develop and sustain such structures and, moreover, to facilitate their proper use. This requires breaking down artificial barriers to sympathetic communication and educating individuals for those skills and traits of character peculiarly consonant with democratic institutions. Of all the freedoms required by such institutions, freedom of mind is basic, for, without it, individuals are not genuinely free do develop. "Freed intelligence," says Dewey, "is necessary to direct and to warrant freedom of action."[6] It is the cultivation of free, sympathetic, and critical intelligence that constitutes at once the fundamental imperative of democracy and the main task of its education.

The foregoing sketch of pragmatic ideas provides at best a general and composite picture rather than an individual portrait of any single pragmatist. I shall therefore devote the remainder of my remarks to the pioneering work of Charles Sanders Peirce, the founder of the movement, focusing, in particular, upon his rejection of Descartes and the development of his influential alternative theory of belief, doubt, and inquiry.

2. Peirce's Theory of Belief, Doubt, and Inquiry

In place of Descartes's emphasis on *radical doubt* and Locke's emphasis on *sensations*, Peirce emphasizes *belief*, indeed placing the notion of belief at the center of his theory of inquiry. Thought, or inquiry, arises always in a context of belief and it is precipitated by doubt. Doubt is, however, not the mere lack of belief; it is an active state of irritation, focused and specific rather than wholesale and diffuse like the Cartesian variety. Provoked by such irritation, inquiry arises, inquiry being the active process of passing from doubt to belief. Unlike doubt, belief is itself a calm, settled state of readiness, in the nature of a habit; it is not an episode or occurrence but more like a disposition or set. In Alexander Bain's words, it is that upon which we are prepared to act. Orienting us thus to future experience, belief is always, in consequence, open to upset by experience. Certainty of belief is therefore precluded. Indeed, since belief is expressible only in signs, with implicit reference to other signs, it is always mediated and never direct, hence in principle incapable of certainty. "From the proposition that every thought is a sign," says Peirce, "it follows that every thought must address itself to some other, must determine some other, since that is the essence of a sign."[7] All thoughts are thus in the same boat, all fallible, all interdependent. In place of Cartesian certainty, Peirce in fact espouses rather what he calls *fallibilism*.

The underpinnings of these ideas are developed in two papers of 1868, both devoted to criticism of Descartes. In the first of these, "Questions Concerning Certain Faculties Claimed for Man," Peirce criticizes the doctrine of intuition or immediate knowledge. In the second, "Some Consequences of Four Incapacities," he concentrates on issues of logic and methodology. "We cannot," he says in the latter paper, "begin with complete doubt" since doubt requires a positive reason. Even in philosophy, this principle ought to hold. "Let us not pretend to doubt in philosophy what we do not doubt in our hearts."[8] Radical Cartesian doubt, since it is in fact impossible, must be empty and self-deceptive. Its impotence is revealed by the fact that the Cartesian method that begins with radical doubt ends by recovering all the beliefs with which the doubter began. Real doubt, on the other hand, as illustrated by a typical research question in the sciences is focused and motivated, framed by a variety of assumptions meanwhile taken for granted. Such doubt is not impotent; it has, indeed, the power to stimulate inquiry that may in the end alter the beliefs of the doubter. Each provisional assumption may, furthermore, be doubted in its turn, but at no time are *all* assumptions thrown into doubt at once.

Peirce considered Alexander Bain's definition of belief as "that upon which a man is prepared to act" as the basis of his pragmatism.[9] Bain's view, as Murphey suggests, supplied the "psychological foundation for Peirce's denial of Cartesian doubt, for Bain holds that men are naturally believers and that doubt is produced only by events which disrupt our beliefs—not by pretense."[10] Rather than supposing that the "natural" state is utter lack of belief, i.e., *radical doubt*, so that every belief we have requires justification from scratch, Bain offers Peirce a theory that reverses the order of naturalness, as the modern concept of inertia reversed the natural state from rest to motion. The natural psychological state is now held to be that of belief with no possibility of wholesale and radical justification. Rather, doubt arising in the body of our beliefs now wants a positive reason, and it finds resolution in the recapture of belief. Using Bain's idea, Peirce can, as Murphey points out,

> fit his whole theory of inquiry into an evolutionary frame of reference. Beliefs may be regarded as adjustive habits while failure of adjustment leads to doubt. . . . This biological perspective . . . provides him with a new definition of the nature of a problem—a definition subsequently developed by Dewey. A problem situation exists whenever we find our established habits of conduct inadequate to attain a desired end, . . . and the effect of a problem situation upon us is the production of doubt. This being the case, Cartesian doubt is nonsense, for there is no problem situation. But secondly, the theory provides a clarification of the nature of an answer. An answer is any rule of action which enables us to attain our desired ends. Accordingly, our objective is to find a rule which will always lead us to that which we desire. So in the investigation of a real object, our objective is a knowledge of how to act respecting that object so as to attain our desired ends. Thus, as pragmatism asserts, the concept of the object can mean nothing to us but all the habits

it involves. The attainment of a stable belief—belief that will stand in the long run—is thus the goal of inquiry. Such belief we define as true and its objects as reality.[11]

In his 1877 paper "The Fixation of Belief," Peirce presents a full statement of his theory. Doubt differs from belief in three respects, he says. First, "there is a dissimilarity between the sensation of doubting and that of believing"; second, "the feeling of believing is a more or less sure indication of there being established in our nature some habit which will determine our actions. Doubt never has such an effect"; and third, "doubt is an uneasy and dissatisfied state from which we struggle to free ourselves and pass into the state of belief, while the latter is a calm and satisfactory state which we do not wish to avoid, or to change to a belief in anything else. On the contrary, we cling tenaciously, not merely to believing, but to believing just what we do believe."[12]

Inquiry, now, is the struggle to overcome doubt and attain belief, and it has in doubt its "only immediate motive." It begins with doubt and ends only with the cessation of doubt. Therefore, says Peirce, "The sole object of inquiry is the settlement of opinion." When opinion is settled and "real and living doubt" overcome, genuine inquiry cannot arise. When no *actual* doubt affects any given proposition, it does not matter that it might *possibly* be thrown into doubt by hypothetical considerations.

3. Peirce's Comparison of Methods

If the function of inquiry is indeed the settlement of opinion, or the fixation of belief, the question may be raised as to the relative effectiveness of alternative methods by which this function may be carried out. Considering this question, Peirce proceeds to a comparison of four such methods: the method of tenacity, the method of authority, the a priori method, and the method of science. Simple tenacity, i.e., a reiteration of the belief, "dwelling on all which may conduce to that belief, and learning to turn with contempt and hatred from anything which might disturb it" is a method "really pursued by many men" and offering "great peace of mind" despite some inconveniences. But it is ineffective for, as Peirce says, "the social impulse is against it." Finding oneself confronted with the differing opinions of others, one's confidence in one's own tenaciously held beliefs is shaken. Nor can we shield ourselves from contacts with others unless we become hermits. Tenacity thus leaves us vulnerable to continual unsettlement of our beliefs.

The method of authority, transferring tenacity to the group, utilizes social or political institutions to inculcate preferred doctrines and to stamp out contrary views. A whole array of repressive measures is available, e.g., censorship, indoctrination, terror, with occasional massacres as needed, for, as Peirce remarks, these have proved "very effective means of settling opinion in a country." The method of authority is capable of atrocity for, says Peirce, "the officer of a society does not feel justified in surrendering the interests of that society for the sake of mercy, as he might his own private interests." As to effectiveness, authority is superior to tenacity, shielding the individual, by and large, from encounters with differing opinions. But is has its own sources of inefficiency nevertheless: social regulation cannot extend to all opinions whatever, and unregulated opinion always poses a potential threat to settled belief. Individuals may reflect that other societies and other ages have held quite different beliefs, and conclude that it is mere historical accident that has led them to the official doctrines they have. Such doubts must, says Peirce, affect "every belief which seems to be determined by the caprice either of themselves or of those who originated the popular opinions."

The a priori method rejects tenacity as well as the effort to force one's beliefs on others. Rather, it follows the natural preferences of "men conversing together and regarding matters in different lights." The chief example of the operation of this method is to be found in "the history of metaphysical philosophy, "where beliefs have been formed not in the effort to account for observed facts but rather in the effort to formulate what seemed "agreeable to reason." Enjoying greater intellectual respectability than either of the others already considered, this method nevertheless fails equally. It is ineffective since it assimilates inquiry to the development of taste, always a matter of fashion, and thus never culminates in agreement but remains always subject to pendulum swings over time. When we reflect on the diversity of fashion, we recognize our own beliefs to have been formed by such "accidental causes," and new doubts arise again to unsettle these beliefs.

The method of science, finally, is one that purports to form beliefs by reference to external permanencies rather than human causes. It supposes real things with properties "entirely independent of our opinions about them." It is true, says Peirce, that the supposition of realities cannot be proved by science, since it *underlies* science, but practice of the scientific method never leads us to doubt this supposition, whereas practice of the other methods does lead us to doubt them. To question the existence of real things *in general* is idle: "If there be anybody with a living doubt upon the subject," says Peirce, "let him consider it." But the fundamental contrast between the method of science and all the others is that it is the only one that presents "any distinction of a right and a wrong way." The method, that is to say, is self-corrective, acknowledging the possibility of errors in application corrigible by further use of the method itself. By contrast, the result of applying any of the other methods is necessarily correct according to the method in question, so that no errors can be admitted, much less corrected, by the method itself. While the other methods have their virtues, a man should reflect, says Peirce, that "after all, he wishes his opinions to coincide with the fact, and that there is no reason why the results of those first three methods should do so. To bring about this effect is the prerogative of the method of science."

4. Difficulties in Peirce's Treatment

The doubt–belief theory of inquiry is central to Peirce's general conceptions of mind, meaning, truth, and reality. It appealed to him in the first instance as providing a psychological foundation for his epistemological critique of Descartes. Read purely as psychology, it seems to me, however, obscure on several points, which I have elaborated more fully in my book *Four Pragmatists*. For example, is doubt always conscious or may it simply be inferred from its characteristic disruptive effects on conduct? Although described as an occurrent state of irritation, it might still theoretically be construed as not implying consciousness in every case; yet Peirce affirms a "sensation of doubting." Does he then call the characteristic disruptive effects minus the characteristic sensation "doubt" or not? The answer is unclear.

To take another example, how, if belief is a habit or set, can Peirce speak of a "sensation of believing" and describe it (in the companion essay "How to Make Our Ideas Clear") as "something we are aware of"? More important, how can he say of belief (in this same essay) that it "appeases the irritation of doubt," having earlier argued that belief is prior to doubt, constituting indeed the natural state of the mind before inquiry. Finally, what does Peirce intend in saying that belief involves the establishment of a rule of action or a habit? Since not all habits are associated with beliefs, does he have any way of specifying which subclass of habits is peculiarly belief-related? Does he, similarly, have any way of indicating which disruptions of conduct are constitutive of doubt? To me, at any rate, these unanswered questions indicate basic obscurities in the theory, under a psychological interpretation.

However, the theory may be given an *epistemological* rather than a *psychological* interpretation; taken thus, it is not necessarily vulnerable to the difficulties just outlined, and it requires a fresh evaluation. Interpreted epistemologically, the theory purports not to *describe* but rather to *prescribe* the course of thought, construed as a critical or scientific effort. Properly, the theory declares, such thought always addresses specific questions arising from real doubt, proceeding in every case by taking a variety of assumptions for granted throughout the inquiry, and subject to evaluation by seeing how well it turns out to resolve the questions from which it arose. The theory thus rejects the idea that there can be scientific investigations without assumptions altogether, and it equally rejects the idea that assumptions actually adopted must be absolutely indubitable.

Although this epistemological version of the theory does indeed escape the problems of the psychological reading, Peirce's insistence on "real and living doubt" as the proper origin of inquiry still poses a difficulty. For there is, in fact, much thinking of a significant kind that does not originate in doubt. Imagination, recollection, perception, translation, composition—all seem to provide counterinstances. In reply, it will be said that Peirce is concerned, not with thinking in general, but with *inquiry* specifically, in particular as exemplified in scientific research. Is it then the case that all such research originates, or should originate, in real and living doubt? Does there really need to be an active irritation, a breakdown in earlier habits, before scientific research can be initiated? Does not theoretical curiosity have a role in the stimulation of inquiry? Peirce insists, to the contrary, that genuine thought arises from real and active irritation rather than from theoretical or speculative motives.

Nevertheless, he displays increasing ambivalence on this central point. As early as 1878, in "How to Make Our Ideas Clear," he speaks of "feigned hesitancy," saying that "whether feigned for mere amusement or with a lofty purpose," it "plays a great part in the production of scientific inquiry."[13] Then, in a note added in 1893 to "The Fixation of Belief," he states that doubt is typically "anticipated hesitancy about what I shall do hereafter, or a feigned hesitancy about a fictitious state of things. It is the power of making believe we hesitate, together with the pregnant fact that the decision upon the merely make-believe dilemma goes toward forming a bona fide habit that will be operative in a real emergency."[14] Finally, in a note of 1903, he says that "for the sake of the pleasures of inquiry, men may like to seek out doubts.[15] The net effect of these qualifications is surely to deny that research must always spring from actual difficulties, real irritations, or living doubts; it is also to acknowledge that the researcher is motivated not only to solve problems but to seek them. Research activity, in sum, does not subside when real doubts are dispelled, real problems resolved—for the generation of feigned doubts and hypothetical problems continues unabated.

Peirce's theory of inquiry, even under epistemological interpretation, thus remains difficult. In its unqualified form, it clashes with the fact of theoretical motivation in research. Taken together with its supplementary qualifications, it appears inconsistent. The qualified theory, moreover, undercuts Peirce's earlier criticism of Descartes. For, having himself insisted on the role of feigned or hypothetical doubt in science, how can Peirce dismiss Descartes's radical doubt as mere idle pretense?

5. An Epistemological Interpretation

My own view is that Peirce's formulation, *that all inquiry must begin in real and living doubt*, is indeed untenable. It implies that without real and living doubt there can be no inquiry; yet Peirce admits the importance of inquiries springing from doubts that are merely feigned. Once feigned inquiries are admitted, however, what differentiates Peirce's notion of doubt from the radical doubt of Descartes? What is the distinctive import of Peirce's theory?

I suggest the answer lies in the *role* ascribed to feigned doubt. For Descartes's method, feigned doubt disqualifies a proposition from serving as an assumption, since what he seeks are assumptions not only undoubted but indubitable. For Peirce, on the other hand, a proposition that is as a matter of fact undoubted, i.e., free of real and living doubt, still qualifies as an assumption, even though subject to feigned doubt. The mere fact that one might *hypothetically* doubt such a proposition does not *require* us to reject it as an assumption and try to replace it, or perhaps reinstate it through additional argumentation. We are *required* to disqualify assumptions only if they are subject to real and living doubts—that is, doubts that are specific to the propositions in question and that rest on positive reasons. But a proposition we are not *required* to reject as an assumption may be rejected anyhow for the space of a given hypothetical inquiry, during which other undoubted assumptions are meanwhile retained. Inquiries may, in other words, indeed originate in feigned doubt; such feigning is consistent with use of the proposition in question as an assumption in other inquiries; the mere possibility of such feigning does not render assumptions generally useless. Peirce, according to this interpretation, is here rejecting the unconditional or wholesale doubt of radical skepticism, insisting that inquiry may stand on undoubted although dubitable assumptions, even as it proceeds to investigate others taken as problematic. The skeptic, doubting all assumptions short of indubitability, leaves himself no room to stand and allows himself no resources for dealing with the problems he raises. He errs, not in his feigning as such but in his demand that all hypothetically dubitable propositions be simultaneously feigned to be useless as assumptions. By contrast, scientific doubt, whether it is real or feigned, is always specific, resting on provisional assumptions that serve usefully as premises of the inquiry even though they fall short of absolute certainty. Nor is the scientific researcher's work done when his problem is solved, for he will then try to find, imagine, or construct new problems specific enough to be formulable as testable questions. The answer to the skeptical yearning for certainty at the outset thus lies in the continuity of fallible inquiries tending toward the fixation of beliefs in the future.

6. The Primacy of Method

Consider now Peirce's comparison of methods in "The Fixation of Belief," a comparison that is very puzzling indeed. For Peirce promises to compare his four methods solely by reference to their relative effectiveness in stabilizing belief since, as he says, "the settlement of opinion is the sole object of inquiry." Yet, in defending the method of science, he does not even mention its superior effectiveness, but invokes instead a variety of new considerations, some metaphysical (relating to the supposition of real things), some methodological (relating to self-correctiveness), some epistemological (relating to the need for opinions to aspire to coincidence with fact), and some even moral ("to avoid looking into the support of any belief from a fear that it may turn out rotten is quite as immoral as it is disadvantageous").

Moreover, to defend science as more successful than the other methods in settling belief seems doomed to failure anyhow. Science does not, like the method of tenacity, yield "great peace of mind." Indeed the rate of change of scientific opinions would seem to be higher than that associated with any of the other methods. What is characteristic of science is that it places all its claims in perpetual jeopardy, making them forever vulnerable to unsettlement. It might perhaps be thought plausible to defend scientific method through appeal to the restless spirit of man, relishing the prospect of a continued unfixing of beliefs and recasting of received doctrines. How could Peirce have hoped to succeed in the exactly opposite course?

Perhaps, it might be said, the mere *change* of scientific opinion is not fatal to the notion of science as stabilizing belief. For such change may be construed as uniformly *progressive*, i.e., as adding to reliable information without disturbing the already available stock, as sharpening the vaguer formulations of the past, or as steadily narrowing the range of opinion in a process of approximation to an ideal limit. Such a conception is reflected in the important passage in "How to Make Our Ideas Clear" in which Peirce says that truth is "the opinion which is fated to be ultimately agreed to by all who investigate . . . , and the object represented in this opinion is the real." Scientists, he says, "may at first obtain different results, but, as each perfects his method and his processes, the results will move steadily together toward a destined center."[16]

This idea is, however, vulnerable to two criticisms. First, the concept of approximation may be suitable for measurements, but it does not fit theories. As Quine has remarked, "the notion of limit depends on that of 'nearer than,' which is defined for numbers and not for theories."[17] Second, science does not simply add information or sharpen vague formulations or steadily converge in opinion; it often changes theoretical direction and rejects previous beliefs. Even if experimental and technological knowledge *does* tend to accumulate, even if later theories, in accounting for a wider range of such knowledge, are considered not merely *different from* but *superior to* earlier theories, still theoretical change must be recognized to be non-progressive: the theoretical agreement of a given period is often uprooted and superseded by a *conflicting* agreement in a later period. And this is incompatible with the project of showing science to be maximally effective in *fixing beliefs in general*. It is perhaps, I conjecture, some such train of thought that accounts for the first difficulty with the essay, i.e., that the defense of the method of science shifts ground, moving from a consideration of effectiveness to other considerations of various sorts.

These latter considerations have this in common: they transfer attention from the stability of *particular beliefs* to that of *methods*, arguing that the method of science is *itself* firmer than the other methods discussed. Because it rests on the undoubted supposition of real things, because it is self-corrective, because it tests beliefs not by reference to human attitudes, intuitions, or institutions but rather by reference to those facts to which the beliefs purport to refer, scientific method is itself capable of standing firm through the change of specific beliefs. To challenge a particular belief sanctioned by any of the other methods calls the method itself into question because none of these methods is capable of allowing consistent correction of its own pronouncements. These methods are *brittle*, incapable of absorbing change without fracture. The method of science, by contrast, achieves stability through flexibility. Rejecting pretensions to certainty, opening wide the testing process to all members of the ideal community of investigators, requiring continual correction to account for all available facts, the method is itself capable of absorbing change without upset. Since, however, the essay thus shifts the question of stability from the level of belief to that of method, it does not in fact fulfill its promise. Yet the defense of science it offers is of interest in its own right, exemplifying, moreover, that emphasis on the primacy of method that is characteristic of pragmatic philosophy in all its variants. It is method rather than doctrine that defines the community of investigation, and it is the stability of method in pursuit of the truth that holds this community together throughout doctrinal change. Similarly, for pragmatic social theory, it is the method embodied in democratic institutions that defines the community dedicated to the qualities of human freedom and dignity, and it is the stability of democratic methods that may hold the community together through changes of policy and belief.

The task of education, finally, is to teach proper method. Its special function, as Dewey emphasized, is not to indoctrinate a particular point of view but rather to develop those powers of logical assessment and criticism by which diverse points of view may themselves be evaluated.

Method, moreover, is the key to intellectual advance, and education therefore has another powerful motivation to stress method as primary. It is this aspect of education to which Peirce attaches the greatest importance. Construing logic as a methodical study of methods, and associating it with the general theory of signs, he writes: "When new paths have to be struck out, a spinal cord is not enough; a brain is needed, and that brain an organ of mind, and that mind perfected by a liberal education. And a liberal education—so far as its relation to the understanding goes—means *logic*."[18]

Notes

1   Murray G. Murphey, "Kant's Children: The Cambridge Pragmatists," *Transactions of the Charles S. Peirce Society* 4 (1968): 3–33.

2   Max H. Fisch, *Classic American Philosophers* (New York: Appleton-Century-Crofts, 1951, 1966), preface and general introduction.

3   Gail Kennedy, "Introduction to John Dewey," in Fisch, *Classic American Philosophers*, pp. 328–29.

4   See Fisch, "The Classic Period in American Philosophy," in Fisch, *Classic American Philosophers*, pp. 10–12.

5   John Dewey, *The Quest for Certainty* (New York: Minton, Balch, & Co., 1929), p. 151; William James, *Collected Essays and Reviews* (New York: Longmans, Green, 1920), pp. 86–87; quoted in Fisch, *Classic American Philosophers*, p. 26; and Dewey, *The Quest for Certainty*, p. 213.

6   John Dewey, "Democracy and Educational Administration," *School and Society* (1937): 457–62; reprinted in Ratner, *Intelligence in the Modern World* (New York: Modern Library, 1939), p. 404.

7   C. S. Peirce, "Questions Concerning Certain Faculties Claimed for Man," in *Collected Papers of Charles Sanders Peirce*, Charles Hartshorne and Paul Weiss, eds. (Cambridge, MA: Harvard University Press), 5.253.

8   Ibid., 5.265.

9   Ibid., 5.12–13.

10   Murray G. Murphey, *The Development of Peirce's Philosophy* (Cambridge, MA: Harvard University Press, 1961), p. 161.

11   Ibid., p. 163.

12   Peirce, *Collected Papers*, 5:370 ff.

13   Ibid., 5.394.

14   Ibid., 5.373, n. l.

15   Ibid., 5.372, n. 2.

16   Ibid., 5.407.

17 W. V. Quine, *Word and Object* (New York: Technology Press of MIT and John Wiley, 1960), p. 23.

18 From the *Johns Hopkins University Circulars* (November 1882) as excerpted by M. H. Fisch and J. I. Cope, "Peirce at the Johns Hopkins University," in *Studies in the Philosophy of C. S. Peirce*, Philip P. Wiener and Frederic H. Young, eds. (Cambridge, MA: Harvard University Press, 1952), pp. 289–90, reprinted in Wiener, *C. S. Peirce: Selected Writings* (New York: Dover, 1958), pp. 336–37.

Chapter 5

Action and Commitment[1]

The idea of justification is one of the keys to normative ethics. To say of some act that it is right, warranted, or valid, is to say that it is justified.* To predicate goodness of something is to hold its approval justified. To describe an act as obligatory is to say not only that it is justified but also that there is no feasible alternative equally justified. Understanding justification, then, we are in a position to unlock some of the rustiest and most heavily bolted doors in ethical theory. I want, in what follows, to propose an interpretation of this key idea.

What we ordinarily may be said to justify, strictly, are actions, deliberate moves, controllable act-patterns, items of our behavior for which we are responsible. Indeed, justification does not apply to anything for which no one is responsible, while to be responsible for something is just to be subject to the demand for its justification. Since what we are, strictly, responsible for is our controllable behavior, what we are called upon to justify is such behavior. The apparent exception as regards the justification of cognitive statements is a real exception only if we split cognition from action, and deny that belief, affirmation, and assertion are kinds of deliberate behavior, for which we are responsible. As a matter of fact, a study of the justification of cognitive belief, affirmation, or sentence-acceptance turns out to be illuminating for all cases of justification.

How then do we justify the acceptance of some sentence, A? Coherence of A with some system of sentences, in the sense of derivability or inclusion within the system, is not sufficient, for the negation of A is also coherent with some system, though the systems with which A and −A, respectively,

* This chapter originally appeared as "On Justification and Commitment," *Journal of Philosophy* 51 (1954): 180–90.

are coherent are mutually incompatible, if consistent. Clearly we need some way of choosing, among internally coherent but mutually incompatible systems, one which is to serve as a standard system. The correspondence of A with fact is equally unsatisfactory as a description of what is essential to cognitive justification. It is unclear what it means for a statement to correspond with fact; moreover, no matter how we agree to understand it, it is not likely to be sufficient either, for the most conscientiously corresponding statement has systematic import, i.e., is subject to withdrawal under pressure from incompatible sister statements which we happen to be interested in saving. Somehow, it seems, we need to supplement coherence with correspondence in such a way that correspondence will select a standard system which will, in turn, represent just those sentences with which A must come to terms, or cohere.

A proposal for doing just this was recently suggested by Professor Goodman in another connection, during the course of a discussion of empirical certainty.[2] Agreeing with Professor Lewis that probability with respect to certain premises is never sufficient to render any sentence credible, Goodman argues that no sentence need nevertheless be certain; it need only have some degree of underived or initial credibility. The correspondence factor, that is, may be minimally conceived as some degree of initial credibility attaching to sentences. Yet no sentence is ever immune from withdrawal, or, what amounts to the same thing, is a necessarily fixed description of any particular fact of experience. Thus, the sentence "There is now a sheet of paper before me" is highly credible but may be replaced, if need arises, by any of a number of other sentences with lower initial credibility, provided there is a total gain. Choice among internally coherent, mutually incompatible systems is accomplished, that is, by noting which of them maximizes initial credibility. The justification for accepting A at a given time may now be made not on the grounds of its own initial credibility, nor of some unspecified coherence, but on the basis of its coherence with the system which maximizes initial credibility at that time, while, together with its sister sentences, A indirectly controls the choice of this standard system. Circularity is avoided because, whereas it is each single sentence which is judged by coherence, it is the totality of sentences which exercises control by correspondence, or initial credibility.

An example or two may help to clarify this conception. Suppose we have two incompatible sentences differing in initial credibility, both independent of our heretofore standard system, both seeking entry to the system. Our choice will go to the sentence with higher initial credibility, not by consideration of these two sentences alone, but by anticipation of systematic effect, i.e., because the opposite choice would mean a lower total credibility value for our standard system.

Of course, since no sentence is a necessary description of a given experience, neither are we ever limited to just two alternatives. We may have an indefinite number of applicants vying for entry to the system. We may, if we like, consider every sentence as a candidate for inclusion, since every sentence may trivially be said to have some degree, perhaps zero, or a negative value, of initial credibility. As initial credibility rises, the temptation to add to our total credibility by a simple inclusion of the sentence increases. But no matter how urgent it becomes, it is counterbalanced by the demand that the total system must not be lowered in credibility by the repercussions of such inclusion. Whether, then, we consider two or an indefinite number of candidates for inclusion, systematic consequences for total credibility are dominant in our inclusion-policy.

Not only are all sentences short of certainty, but the degree of their initial credibility is subject to change over time. Let us take, as a simplified illustration of such change, a case of systematic overhauling precipitated by a disconfirming crucial experiment. At time t_1, before the experiment, one of the sentences, Z, deductively entailed by a given theory and hence part of the system including it, has a given degree of initial credibility. At time t_2, following the experiment, $-Z$ jumps high in credibility, while Z drops drastically. The resulting choice is often a complicated one. Including the negate and revising the system internally may increase the latter's credibility in this area, but has repercussions in other areas where accompanying theoretical revision, in the interests of coherence, demands a reshuffling of sentences. In addition, pragmatic factors of inertia, convenience, and simplicity must be taken into account. It is clear, nevertheless, that if maintaining the system intact jeopardizes its total credibility, a drastic overhauling is indicated. Now, a systematic overhauling, though heightening the total credibility, may oust some sentences with higher initial credibilities in favor of counterparts with lower. The acceptance of the latter is justified clearly not on the basis of their own isolated merits but rather on the basis of their systematic connections.

Summing up the discussion so far, then, we justify the acceptance of A at time t by showing that A belongs to the maximally credible system of sentences at time t; we justify accepting a particular system at time t by showing that its total credibility value at time t is not less than that of any of its contemporary rivals. Since A exercises partial control over choice of the standard system, moreover, its coherence with the latter must not be construed as a passive meshing with any systematic status quo. A may fail to cohere with the accepted system at a given time, and help to force a drastic overhauling and a change in system-acceptance.

So far I have spoken of the justification of sentence-acceptances and of system-acceptances, and have used the notion of coherence rather uncritically. It may be said, however, that the coherence-rules of a system, though not themselves systematic sentences but rather extra-systematic devices, need justification for their acceptance as well, since they exercise some control over admission of sentences. As Professor Quine points out, though they may be altered reluctantly or perhaps never, they are theoretically always subject to modification. Our examples show just how changes in the requirements of coherence might be useful. We spoke of choice among incompatible sentences or systems. Now a weakening of the rules of incompatibility might always be made in such a way as to eliminate the need for choice, and enable us to dispose of all such problems trivially, were it not for the fact that we have compunctions about changing rules. Now the fact that these compunctions operate to prevent our solving all problems by weakening the rules of the game, though we may solve some of our problems in this way, shows that rule-acceptance requires justification too, that rules are rationally controlled though credibility is inapplicable to them.

I think that pragmatic considerations are as relevant here as elsewhere. Some rules are more habitual, seem more natural, more economical of effort than others. However, I think that for rules as well as systems, initial sentence-credibility exercises considerable control. If one set of rules, roughly speaking, admits fewer low-credibility sentences than another, it is preferable, other things being equal. Abandoning a given coherence requirement, for example, to accommodate two erstwhile incompatible sentences we should like to save, we may lower the total credibility value of our system by admitting a host of undesirable sentences otherwise excluded. Thus, rules may be said to be justified to the degree in which they maximize credibility in the systems in which they are applied.

It will be recalled that I began by limiting the notion of justifiedness to deliberate, responsible behavior. Now I should not like to be misunderstood as denying that, in ordinary discourse, we often do speak of justifying sentences, or, for that matter, of being responsible for some object, situation, or other non-behavioral entity. I am suggesting, however, that this mode of speech is an extension, that we are, strictly speaking, not responsible for the situation, but for our behavior in bringing it about or preserving it; that we, correspondingly, do not justify sentences, but rather sentence-acceptances. Independent evidence for this suggestion is, perhaps, afforded by the fact that, even in ordinary discourse, we do not speak of responsibility for anything to which our action is considered to lack the appropriate relation of bringing about, contributing toward, or helping to preserve.

As a matter of fact, this suggestion accords well with familiar ethical tradition. Together with responsibility for our controllable, deliberate behavior go sanctions directed toward a selective nurturing of some kinds of action as over against others; responsibility of the agent derives its meaning from the significance of certain of his actions. If I am right in supposing that we may not properly be said to justify anything which imposes no responsibility, then only our deliberate behavior is properly justifiable, while apparently contrary locutions may be construed as extensions. The parallelism is strengthened by our speaking, ordinarily, not only of the justifiedness of some entity simply, but also of an agent's justifiedness in performing some act, just as we speak of an agent's responsibility for some act.

Justification is, then, I should say, in every case applied to behavior, because we are vitally interested in the control of behavior and the classification which facilitates control. Interested in controlling the future history of sentence-acceptance, we justify sentence-acceptances, not sentences. Understandably, however, we extend the notion of justification to the latter because of their close relations to sentence-acceptances. Some reflections on these relations will perhaps serve to clarify the present conception.

According to our previous discussion, the acceptance of A at time t is justified if A belongs to the maximally credible system of sentences at time t. Now it is obviously not necessary that, for every sentence, S, which belongs to this system, there should in actual historical fact be an S-acceptance, though every sentence-acceptance involves a sentence. Thus, we can refer to any actual sentence-acceptance by reference to a corresponding sentence, although not conversely, even for sentences included in the maximally credible set. Furthermore, if inclusion in this set be termed "groundedness," then justifying an acceptance will always involve reference to a corresponding, grounded sentence, while showing that a sentence is grounded will not always imply that there is, in point of fact, a corresponding, justified acceptance. Justification, then, should be distinguished from groundedness, and reserved for application to behavioral entities. Since each act of justified sentence-acceptance is, however, connected to a grounded sentence, we may refer to each act by way of its associated sentence, while the utility of such reference, as contrasted with an independent psychological description of the act, is a precision, a specificity, a stability otherwise unattainable. The transfer of the notion of justification from affirmations to sentences is, then, reasonable, convenient, and harmless for the most part.

I have, however, dwelt at some length upon this apparently unimportant point because the close connection between sentence-grounding and affirmation-justification has led to understandable confusion of the two, and has caused considerable trouble in the study of ethical and legal justification. On the one hand, those anxious to avoid subjectivism in ethics and to treat ethics cognitively seek a general notion of justification in terms of sentences. Just as science justifies sentences, so, it is thought, ethics must justify sentences if it is to be objective. On the other hand, opponents of this position, in an effort to account for the tie-up of ethics with action and to deny this parallelism with science, feel that they must deny ethical objectivity altogether, as well as the cognitive nature of ethical judgment. The first group says, in effect, "If ethics is to be objective, its goal must be a system of justified sentences." The second group retorts, in effect, "Since ethics is concerned with action, and hence not with a listing of justified sentences, it can itself be no more than action, a form of non-cognitive stimulation."

Actually, it seems to me that both arguments are non sequiturs. Even if we grant, for the moment, that justifiedness is attributable to sentences, we do not thereby deny that it may also hold of acts. If so, the goal of ethics may be a listing of justified acts, just as that of science is a listing of justified sentences; ethics can be cognitive and objective though concerned with action. On the further assumption of this paper that justifiedness is never properly applicable to sentences at all, and that it is to be distinguished from groundability, this confused dilemma between sentential non-activism and active non-cognitivism never arises. Furthermore, a new, pervasive parallel unites the realms of cognition and action. Cognition is a kind of action, and justifiability applies to the one as it does to the other.

If I am not mistaken in thinking that justification is of behavior in the interests of control, that in cognitive justification we are interested in controlling acceptance of grounded sentences, and that we refer to such acts by way of their linguistic counterparts to achieve stability and descriptive precision, a number of features in the landscape of our problem begin to take on more definite form. It becomes clear that while justification may have the same general features and motivation when what are justified are not acceptance-acts, nevertheless, because these other acts have no relatively stable and precise linguistic counterparts, we lack what appears to be the best way presently available for characterizing them. We are reduced to characterizing them in both motivational and socio-cultural terms, and both these ways are presently more primitive, more complex, and more evanescent than description by way of linguistic relations. Thus, though the justificational pattern is constant, we may expect at the outset a tremendously greater amount of vagueness and fogginess in ethico-legal justification simply because we have no well-developed referential scheme. Our difficulties in denoting and classifying non-affirmational acts mean that we are unclear even in specifying what it is we are interested in controlling. It is not that we are perfectly clear about our interests but lack a language. It is rather that, having no precise language, we cannot possibly be clear about our interests. And this is so because interests themselves are not clearly specifiable at present in abstraction from their objects. To the extent that we can't specify these objects, we simply don't know what our interests are. Thus, the transfer from affirmational to non-affirmational justification is bound to involve an increase in vagueness, though the pattern remains constant.

Furthermore, we noted that for acceptance-justification, the necessary and sufficient condition is some maximal pattern of associated sentence-credibility. Where we are dealing with non-affirmational acts, credibility is clearly irrelevant, since attributable to sentences only. Yet the notion of some degree of initial credibility attaching to sentences, which it is our purpose to save the most of in acceptance, is suggestive. For to rank sentences in the order of their initial credibility is to rank them at the same time in the order of our initial commitment to their acceptance. And to save the maximum of initial credibility is to save the maximum of our initial commitment to acceptance. To justify acceptances, we might say, is to follow a sort of psychological inertia, or law of least action. We start with an indefinite number of initial acceptance-commitments of various intensities, and we try to conserve as much of the total as we can. Forced to change our acceptance-pattern, we change in such a way as to continue to preserve a maximum of initial commitment at any given time. The reference to credibility, then, I suggest, is not something ultimate in itself for this context, but serves as an indication of initial acceptance-commitment, just as the reference to sentences serves to characterize acceptance behavior. Finally, the notion of the groundedness of sentences and systems in terms of maximum credibility gives us a way of harmonizing and continually re-equilibrating the totality of our acceptance-commitments in such a way as to conserve the maximum and achieve the greatest stability.

Now if this is true of acceptance-commitments, it may also be true, I suggest, of all sorts of commitment. At any given time, we have all kinds and degrees of committedness to actions and action-patterns at various levels of generality. Our purpose is to harmonize these commitments; to single out, for each moment, a set of acts with maximum initial commitment at that time, which may serve as a standard of justification. I expect to be reminded at this point that there is no law of excluded middle or rule of incompatibility for acts as for sentences, and hence no reason for singling out one standard set of acts, exclusion from which will preclude justification. Without the notion of incompatibility, that is, how can anything be excluded? This, I think, puts the cart before the horse. It is because the degree of credibility of sentence-incompatibles corresponds to the degree of initial commitment to their joint acceptance that we may use the former as a relevant measure of the latter in justifying acceptance. Sentence incompatibility, then, is, in an important sense, a reflection of act-incompatibility. For the sake of clarity, let us reserve the notion of incompatibility for sentences, and speak of acts as being incongruous, to the extent that the initial commitment to their sum is lower than the sum of initial commitments to each singly. The crucial incongruity occurs, of course, when the initial commitment to their sum is lower than each single initial commitment.

We are all familiar with the phenomenon of personal consistency, which makes two acts jointly valueless for us though each singly holds promise. "The philosopher and the lady-killer cannot both keep house in the same tenement of clay," said William James, and I doubt that he meant here to deny the attractiveness of either of these careers, taken singly and pursued consistently. The point here is that, for acts as well as sentences, we cannot simply justify everything if we want to maximize initial commitment, for the incongruity of acts means that a smaller set may have more initial commitment than a larger. While rules of coherence or congruity are justifiable here, as before, to the extent to which they maximize initial commitment, sets of acts are justified when maximal in this respect, and individual acts are justified when they belong to the maximal set. Circularity is avoided here, as before, since, while each act singly is justified by inclusion in the standard act-set, it is the totality of acts which exerts control over the choice of a standard act-set. This description, in terms of commitment, coincides for acceptances with our previous explanation in terms of credibility, as noted, but is generalizable to legal and ethical contexts where credibility is inapplicable.

An important point brought out by this analysis is the systematic import of acts, which forms the basis of ethical and legal justification. Justification is never a question of an isolated act just as it is never a question of an isolated sentence-acceptance, nor is it a non-rational stimulation, as the extreme emotivists would have it. It is the systematic rechanneling of initial commitments in such a way that each act is judged in terms of all others. We do not start from scratch, but always with initial commitments of some degree; but neither do we rest content with the latter. We modify and transform them into derived commitments of various sorts by systematic pressure which is channeled through principles of congruence. These derived commitments to acts, action-patterns, and rules are always changing, yet always subject to control. Whoever looks at ethics through law, or whoever recognizes the complex interplay of initial attraction, derived commitment, and the drive for personal consistency in individual moral choice, will acknowledge the rational and systematic structuring of justification.

The principle of least action operates also in non-affirmational justification. We seek the maximum preservation of initial commitments and make the smallest changes consonant with the continual preservation of this maximum. Legal or ethical reform may involve, however, a kind of systematic overhauling when small changes no longer suffice for maximizing commitment. New social conditions, corresponding in a way to crucial experiments, may radically alter the initial commitments to acts of various kinds, or bring new acts into being which demand taking into account. Radical change in congruence-rules may occur, with a transitional period of unsettlement before a new stability forms. Rapid personal growth may in this way also involve a basic reorientation and new congruence rules.

I may be asked how I justify the maximization of commitment. My answer can only be that I am trying to describe what I take to be the meaning of rational justification. Only a thorough testing of the present proposal will reveal whether or not it is accurate. I cannot further justify the maximization of commitment within my analysis, for on my account such justification is meaningless.

Perhaps a word should be said at this point about the much-debated issue of subjectivity in ethics. On the present account, disagreements over justification are rationally soluble only if initial commitments are constant. Now it is clearly reasonable to assume that degrees of such commitment are assigned differently by different people, and especially by members of different cultures. But this seems to me highly realistic. Legal and ethical outlooks in different cultures may develop justificational schemes which follow the same rational pattern, and yet, since they start from different initial positions, may conflict beyond the possibility of rational adjudication. The same is obviously true of persons within the same cultural environment, or of the same person at different stages of growth. Such subjectivity is not, however, tantamount to the irrationality of the domain of ethics. According to the prevalent stereotype, the rational realm is the realm in which all must eventually come to agree, and the model of such a realm is science. I fail to see, however, what Providence guarantees universal agreement in any domain. Certainly, if the present analysis is correct, subjectivity reigns in the same sense, though perhaps to a lesser degree, in the cognitive or scientific domain, since all justification rests upon initial commitments, which may vary from time to time and from person to person. How to bring a hallucinatory schizophrenic, by rational means, to agree to the truth of physics is, I think, a hopeless problem; one which cannot be decided by defining physics as a rational domain. Rationality, in any event, does not create commitments, but only sets up communication among them, so that we may be guided by a controlled totality, rather than by any single one gone wild. Though disagreements, then, over initial commitments are not rationally soluble, this subjectivity is inevitable in all domains and hence cannot entail a distinguishing irrationality for ethics.

Furthermore, there is a practical factor which offsets the theoretical subjectivity in question. We cannot determine with finality at any given time, regarding any given disagreement, that we have exhausted rational means of adjudication and gotten down to the rock bottom of all relevant initial commitments. Theoretically, we may always continue to expand our attention, originally focused on the circumscribed area of conflict, so that it takes in more and more of the totality of our acts. We may hope to encounter some area of shared commitment, of systematic centrality, such that the original disagreement will be overshadowed. Thus, subjectivity, in the sense indicated, is compatible with a constant practical relevance of shared search for areas of agreement.

Notes

1 Read before the Harvard Philosophical Club on February 19, 1953. I wish to thank Professor N. Goodman, Mr. A. N. Chomsky, and Mr. S. Morgenbesser for helpful comments.
2 N. Goodman, "Sense and Certainty," *Philosophical Review* 61 (April 1952): 160–167.

Chapter 6

Emotion and Cognition

The mention of cognitive emotions may well evoke emotions of perplexity or incredulity.* For cognition and emotion, as everyone knows, are hostile worlds apart. Cognition is sober inspection; it is the scientist's calm apprehension of fact after fact in his relentless pursuit of Truth. Emotion, on the other hand, is commotion—an unruly inner turbulence fatal to such pursuit but finding its own constructive outlets in aesthetic experience and moral or religious commitment.

Strongly entrenched, this opposition of cognition and emotion must nevertheless be challenged for it distorts everything it touches: Mechanizing science, it sentimentalizes art, while portraying ethics and religion as twin swamps of feeling and unreasoned commitment. Education, meanwhile—that is to say, the development of mind and attitudes in the young—is split into two grotesque parts—unfeeling knowledge and mindless arousal. My purpose here is to help overcome the breach by outlining basic aspects of emotion in the cognitive process.

Some misgivings about this purpose will, I hope, be allayed by a preliminary word. My aim, to begin with, is not reductive; I am concerned neither to reduce emotion to cognition nor cognition to emotion—only to show how cognitive functioning employs and incorporates diverse emotional elements—these elements themselves acquiring cognitive significance thereby. I am emphatically not suggesting that cognitions are essentially emotions, or that emotions are, in reality, only cognitions. Nevertheless, I hold that cognition cannot be cleanly sundered from emotion and assigned to science, while emotion is ceded to the arts, ethics, and

* This chapter originally appeared as "In Praise of the Cognitive Emotions," *Teachers College Record* 79, no. 2 (1977): 171–86.

religion. All these spheres of life involve both fact and feeling; they relate to sense as well as sensibility.

Secondly, though applauding the cognitive import of emotions, I do not propose to surrender intellectual controls to wishful thinking, nor shall I portray the heart as giving special access to a higher truth.[1] Control of wishful thinking is utterly essential in cognition; it operates, however, not through an unfeeling faculty of Reason but through the organization of countervailing critical interests in the process of inquiry. These interests of a critical intellect are, in principle, no less emotive in their bearing than those of wayward wish. The heart, in sum, provides no substitute for critical inquiry; it beats in the service of science as well as of private desire.

Finally, I concede it to be undeniable that certain emotional states may be at odds with sound processes of judgment and decision making. Overpowering agitations may derail the course of reasoning; greed, jealousy, or lust may misdirect it; depression or terror may bring it to a total halt. Conversely, the effect of rational judgment may well be to moderate, even wholly to dissipate, certain emotions by falsifying their factual presuppositions: Anger fades, for example, when it turns out the injury was accidental or caused by someone other than first supposed; fear evaporates when the menacing figure becomes the tree's dancing shadow. It does not follow from these cases, however, that emotion as such is uniformly hostile to cognitive endeavors, nor may we properly conclude that cognition is, in general, free of emotional engagement. Indeed, emotion without cognition is blind and, as I shall hope particularly to show in the sequel, cognition without emotion is vacuous.

1. Emotions in the Service of Cognition

Considering now the various roles of emotion in cognition, I divide the field, for convenience, into two main parts, the first having to do with the organization of emotions generally in the service of critical inquiry, and the second having to do with specifically cognitive emotions. Under the first rubric I shall treat: (a) rational passions,[2] (b) perceptive feelings, and (c) theoretical imagination, and I turn first to the rational passions, that is to say, the emotions undergirding the life of reason.

Rational passions

The life of reason is one in which cognitive processes are organized in accord with controlling rational ideals and norms. Such organization involves characteristic patterns of thought, action, and evaluation comprising what may be called rational character. It also thus requires suitable emotional dispositions. It demands, for example, a love of truth and a contempt of lying, a concern for accuracy in observation and inference, and a corresponding repugnance of error in logic or fact. It demands revulsion at distortion, disgust at evasion, admiration of theoretical achievement, respect for the considered arguments of others. Failing such demands, we incur rational shame; fulfilling them makes for rational self-respect.

Like moral character, rational character requires that the right acts and judgments be habitual; it also requires that the right emotions be attached to the right acts and judgments.[3] "A rational man," says R. S. Peters, "cannot, without some special explanation, slap his sides and roar with laughter or shrug his shoulders with indifference if he is told that what he says is irrelevant, that his thinking is confused and inconsistent or that it flies in the face of the evidence."[4] The suitable deployment in conduct of emotional dispositions such as love and hate, contempt and disgust, shame and self-esteem, respect and admiration indeed defines what is meant, quite generally, by the internalization of ideals and principles in character. The wonder is not that rational character is thus related to the emotions but that anyone should ever have supposed it to be an exception to the general rule.

Rational character constitutes an intellectual conscience; it monitors and curbs evasions and distortions; it combats inconsistency, unfairness to the facts, and wishful thinking. In thus exercising control over undesirable impulses, it works for a balance in thought, an epistemic justice, which requires its own special renunciations and develops a characteristic cognitive discipline. There is, however, no question here of the control of impulses through a "bloodless reason,"[5] as control is exercised through the structuring of emotions themselves. Rationality, as John Dewey put it,

> is not a force to evoke against impulse and habit. It is the attainment of a working harmony among diverse desires.... The elaborate systems of

science are born not of reason but of impulses at first slight and flicker-
ing; impulses to handle, move about, to hunt, to uncover, to mix things
separated and divide things combined, to talk and to listen. Method is
their effectual organization into continuous dispositions of inquiry, development and testing. It occurs after these acts and because of their consequences. Reason, the rational attitude, is the resulting disposition. . . .
The man who would intelligently cultivate intelligence will widen,
not narrow, his life of strong impulses while aiming at their happy
coincidence in operation.[6]

This coincidence, I emphasize, requires appropriate organization of
feelings and sentiments in the interests of intelligent control.

Perceptive feelings

Having seen the role of emotions in the internalization of rational
norms, let us consider now their employment in perception. For they are
not only interwoven with our cognitive ideals and evaluative principles;
they are also intimately tied to our vision of the external world. Indeed they
help to construct that vision and to define the critical features of that
world.

These critical features—however specified—are the objects of our evaluative attitudes, the foci of our appraisals of the environment. Our habits
and judgments are keyed in to these appraisals; we define ourselves and
orient our action in the light of our situation as appraised. Characteristic
orientations are associated with distinctive emotional dispositions, and
both involve seeing the environment in a certain light: Is it, for example,
beneficial or harmful, promising or threatening, fulfilling or thwarting?[7]
The subtle and intricate web relating adult feeling and orientation to adult
perception of the environment is a product of evolutionary development,
to be sure, but also of the special circumstances of individual biography.
Acquiring human significance through biographical linkage with critical
features of the environment, our feelings come indeed to signify—to serve
as available cues for interpreting the situation.

Fear of a particular person, for example, presupposes that that person
is regarded as dangerous—danger being a critical feature of the environment calling for a special orientation in response. There need, however,
be no independent evidence, in every case, of the threat we sense: The
characteristic feeling that has become associated for us with past dangers

itself serves us as a cue. Interpreting that feeling as fear, we at once characterize our own state and ascribe danger to the environment. Indeed, we may thence proceed to an explicit attribution of danger, prompted by cues of feeling. Pursuing a more abstract direction in forming our cognitive concepts, we may, further, come to describe a certain situation as terrifying, ascribing to it, independently of our own state, the capacity to arouse fear. Thus employing the emotions as parameters, we gain enormous new powers of fundamental description, while abstracting from actual conditions of feeling.

The notion that aesthetic experience, for example, is peculiarly and purely a matter of emotion ignores such manifold connections of feeling and fact—both fact as embodied in the art work and fact as represented therein. Relative to the latter, H. D. Aiken writes,

> Just as in ordinary circumstances an emotional response is the product of a perceived situation which is apprehended by the individual as promising or threatening, so the expressiveness of an imaginative work arises, at least in part, from the fact that it provides a dramatic representation of an action of which the evoked emotion is the expressive counterpart. And such a representation must be understood as such if the expressive values of the work are to become actual; without it such emotion as the observer might experience would have no ground, and if, by a miracle, it could be sustained, it would still remain the private, dumb, inexpressive importation of the observer himself. As such it would be nothing more than an accidental, adventitious subjective coloring which, having no artistic basis in the thing perceived, would be devoid of aesthetic relevance to it. Aesthetically relevant emotion in art is something which is expressed to us by the action or gesture of the work itself; it is something aroused and sustained by the work as an object for contemplation, and it is found there as a projected quality of the action.[8]

That the emotion is thus tied to a representational understanding of the work of art does not imply, however, that this understanding must be antecedently fashioned, in complete isolation from the feelings. This point must be especially emphasized since the familiar notion of the work of art as "an object for contemplation" may carry contrary, and therefore misleading, connotations. In fact, I believe, the very feelings through which we respond to the content of a work serve us also in interpreting this content. Reading our feelings and reading the work are, in general, virtually inseparable processes.

The cognitive role of the emotions in aesthetic contexts has been emphasized by Nelson Goodman in a recent discussion. He writes,

> The work of art is apprehended through the feelings as well as through the
> senses. Emotional numbness disables here as definitely if not as completely
> as blindness or deafness. Nor are the feelings used exclusively for exploring
> the emotional content of a work. To some extent, we may feel how a painting
> looks as we may see how it feels. The actor or dancer—or the spectator—
> sometimes notes and remembers the feeling of a movement rather than its
> pattern, insofar as the two can be distinguished at all. Emotion in aesthetic
> experience is a means of discerning what properties a work has and
> expresses.[9]

The general point is, of course, not limited to the aesthetic realm since, as
I have earlier emphasized, the emotions intimately mesh with all critical
appraisals of the environment: The flow of feeling thus provides us with a
continuous stream of cues significant for orientation to our changing contexts. Indeed, as Goodman remarks,

> In daily life, classification of things by feeling is often more vital than classi-
> fication by other properties: we are likely to be better off if we are skilled in
> fearing, wanting, braving, or distrusting the right things, animate or inani-
> mate, than if we perceive only their shapes, sizes, weights, etc. And the
> importance of discernment by feeling does not vanish when the motivation
> becomes theoretic rather than practical. . . . Indeed, in any science, while the
> requisite objectivity forbids wishful thinking, prejudicial reading of evi-
> dence, rejection of unwanted results, avoidance of ominous lines of inquiry,
> it does not forbid use of feeling in exploration and discovery, the impetus
> of inspiration and curiosity, or the cues given by excitement over intriguing
> problems and promising hypotheses.[10]

Theoretical imagination

Mention of the context of theory brings us to the third role of emotions in
the service of cognition, that of stimulus to the scientific imagination. This
role is virtually annihilated by the stereotyped emotion–cognition dichotomy. For this dichotomy assigns all feeling and flair, all fantasy and fun,
to the arts and humanities, conceiving the sciences as grim and humorless
grind. The method of science is miserly caution—to gather the facts and

guard the hoard. Imagination is a seductive distraction—a hindrance to serious scientific business.

This doctrine is, in fact, the death of theory. Theory is not reducible to mere fact-gathering, and theoretical creation is beyond the reach of any mechanical routine. Science controls theory by credibility, logic, and simplicity; it does not provide rules for the creation of theoretical ideas. Scientific objectivity demands allegiance to fair controls over theory, but fair controls cannot substitute for ideas. "All our thinking," said Albert Einstein, "is of this nature of a free play with concepts; the justification for this play lying in the measure of survey over the experience of the senses which we are able to achieve with its aid."[11]

The ideal theorist, loyal to the demands of rational character and the institutions of scientific objectivity, is not therefore passionless and prim. Theoretical inventiveness requires not caution but boldness, verve, speculative daring. Imagination is no hindrance but the very life of theory, without which there is no science.

Now the emotions relate to imaginative theorizing in a variety of ways. The emotional life, to begin with, is a rich source of substantive ideas. Drawing from the obscure wellsprings of this life, the mind's free play casts up novel patterns and images, exotic figures and analogies that, in an investigative context, may serve to place old facts in a new light. The dream of the nineteenth-century chemist F. A. Kekulé will provide a striking illustration. He had been trying for a long time to find a structural formula for the benzene molecule. Dozing in front of his fireplace one evening in 1865, he seemed, as he looked into the flames, "to see atoms dancing in snakelike arrays. Suddenly, one of the snakes formed a ring by seizing hold of its own tail and then whirled mockingly before him. Kekulé awoke in a flash: he had hit upon the now famous and familiar idea of representing the molecular structure of benzene by a hexagonal ring. He spent the rest of the night working out the consequences of this hypothesis."[12]

The emotions serve not merely as a source of imaginative patterns; they fulfill also a selective function, facilitating choice among these patterns, defining their salient features, focusing attention accordingly. The patterns developed in imagination, that is, carry their own emotive values; these values guide selection and emphasis. They help imagined patterns to structure the phenomena, highlighting factual features of interest to further inquiry. "Passions," as Michael Polanyi has said, "charge objects with emotions, making them repulsive or attractive; . . . Only a tiny fraction of all

knowable facts are of interest to scientists, and scientific passion serves ...
as a guide in the assessment of what is of higher and what of lesser
interest."[13]

Finally, the emotions play a directive role in the process of applying the
fruits of imagination to the solution of problems. The course of problem-
solving, as has already been intimated, is continually monitored by the
theorist's cues of feeling, his sense of excitement or anticipation, his elation
or suspicion or gloom. Moreover, imagined objects encountered in thought
by the problem-solver affect his deliberation emotively, as real objects do,
and influence his decisions in analogous ways. "In thought as well as in
overt action," says Dewey, "the objects experienced in following out a
course of action attract, repel, satisfy, annoy, promote and retard. Thus
deliberation proceeds."[14] There is, no doubt, much yet to be learned about
the interaction of emotions and imagination in all the ways I have sketched,
and in others as well. It should, however, even now, be evident that creation
is fed by the emotional life in the sphere of science no less than in the
spheres of poetry and the arts.

2. Cognitive Emotions

We have, until now, concerned ourselves with the organization of emotions generally in the service of cognition. I want now to deal with two
emotions that are, in a sense to be explained, specifically cognitive in their
bearing—the joy of verification and the feeling of surprise.

In what sense do I speak of an emotion as specifically cognitive? Consider first the notion of moral emotions, conceived as those resting upon
suppositions of a moral sort: Thus, indignation, for example, rests upon
the supposition of a moral grievance—a piece of injustice, and remorse
presumes that one has in fact done something wrong. If the relevant moral
suppositions are false or lack evidential foundation, the respective emotions may be thought unreasonable, but if these suppositions are not made
at all, that is to say, if the suppositions do not exist, the emotions in question can hardly, in normal circumstances, be said to have occurred. Now
I propose, analogously, to consider an emotion specifically cognitive if it
rests upon a supposition of a cognitive sort—that is to say, a supposition
relating to the content of the subject's cognitions (beliefs, predictions,

expectations) and, in cases of special interest to us, bearing upon their epistemological status.

It is important to avoid misunderstanding of the terminology I have chosen here. It is indeed true that all suppositions may be considered cognitive in a broad sense, inasmuch as they make factual claims expressible in propositional form; moreover, emotions generally, as I have maintained, presuppose the existence of such claims concerning critical features of the environment. However, when I characterize an emotion as specifically cognitive, I mean more than this. In particular, I mean not simply that it presupposes the existence of a factual claim but that the claim in question specifically concerns the nature of the subject's cognitions (and, in cases of interest, is epistemologically relevant to them). A cognitive emotion, I should further emphasize, is thus decidedly an emotion, but an emotion of a certain kind, specifiable by its cognitive reference as just explained.[15]

The joy of verification

In his well-known paper of 1934 on "The Foundation of Knowledge,"[16] Moritz Schlick provides an example of such a cognitive emotion in outlining his theory of science, giving primary place in his theory to the joy that accompanies the fulfillment of an expectation. Cognition, in Schlick's view, has, from the earliest times, always been predictive but the value of reliable prediction lay originally in its practical service to life. "Now in science," he writes, ". . . cognition . . . is not sought because of its utility. With the confirmation of prediction the scientific goal is achieved: the joy in cognition is the joy of verification, the triumphant feeling of having guessed correctly."[17] Such moments of joy are, in Schlick's opinion, of central importance in understanding scientific purpose. "They do not in any way," he says, "lie at the base of science; but like a flame, cognition, as it were, licks out to them, reaching each but for a moment and then at once consuming it. And newly fed and strengthened, it flames onward to the next. These moments of fulfillment and combustion are what is essential. All the light of knowledge comes from them."[18]

Now one need not agree with Schlick's general view of science in order to acknowledge that the satisfaction of a theoretical forecast may indeed occasion joy. Nor is it required that we concur with the extravagant suggestion that all predictive success brings elation. It may, for example, be countered that routine successes based on theory frequently, perhaps typically, go unnoticed, while soberly predicted events may be so dreadful as to occasion not joy but sorrow or despair. Nevertheless, we can agree that the fulfillment of a prediction may indeed crown an investigative achievement in science, producing in its wake what Schlick calls a "triumphant feeling of having guessed correctly."

This joyful feeling I consider a cognitive emotion, because it rests on a supposition (with epistemological relevance) as to the content of the guess in question: It presumes that what has happened is what had, in fact, been predicted. Without such presumption, this joy of verification cannot be said to occur. Whether the presumption is true, or is based on adequate grounds, is another story. Certainly one assumes that the emotion in question may be criticized as unreasonable if it can be shown that what has in fact happened had not, in fact, been predicted.

Can such a criticism, however, actually be entertained as a matter of psychological fact? Is it not, rather, true that our expectations are so powerful as consistently to warp our observations to fit? A whole library of psychological writings testifies to the powerful tendency of expectation to create its own confirmations in experience. The general theme of this testimony may be indicated by the role of normal cues in perception: The perceptual identification of objects "proceeds on the basis of cues normally sufficient to select the objects in question; when these cues fail in fact, we tend anyway to see them as having succeeded."[19] Bruner, Goodnow, and Austin comment on this point as follows:

> If [a bird] has wings and feathers, the bill and legs are highly predictable. In coding or categorizing the environment, one builds up an expectancy of all of these features being present together. It is this unitary conception that has the configurational or Gestalt property of "birdness." Indeed, once a configuration has been established and the object is being identified in terms of configurational attributes, the perceiver will tend to "rectify" or "normalize" any of the original defining attributes that deviate from expectancy. Missing attributes are "filled in" ..., reversals righted ..., colors assimilated to expectancy.[20]

Some philosophers have further maintained that scientific observation itself is systematically theory-laden—presupposing the very theories it is naively thought to test.[21] If indeed we are, as suggested, so blinded by our own theoretical beliefs as to be incapable of acknowledging anything that might contradict them, we can hardly take the joy of verification to represent a cognitive triumph of science. Rather, we must count it an unearned and deluded joy, resulting not from a happy match between theory and experience but solely from our desperate rigging of experience to make it fit.

This conclusion, as I have elsewhere argued, seems to me too extreme for the facts.[22] It is undeniable that our beliefs greatly influence our perceptions, but neither psychology nor philosophy offers any proof of a pre-established harmony between what we believe and what we see. Expectations have the function of orienting us selectively toward the future, but this function does not require that they blind us to the unforeseen. Indeed, the presumption of mismatch between experience and expectation underlies another cognitive emotion: surprise. The existence of this emotion testifies that we are not, in principle, beyond acknowledging the predictive failures of our own theories, that we are not debarred by nature from capitalizing upon such failures in order to learn from experience. The genius of science is, in fact, to institutionalize such learning by wedding the free theoretical imagination to the rigorous probing for predictive failures.

The significance of surprise

Surprise is a cognitive emotion, resting on the (epistemologically relevant) supposition that what has happened conflicts with prior expectation. Without such presumption, surprise cannot be supposed to occur, although the truth of the presumption may, of course, be questioned in particular cases. Surprise must, in any event, not be confused with mere novelty. A novel—that is to say, a hitherto unencountered—contingency may well be anticipated in thought, while a familiar phenomenon, juxtaposed with available theory, may profoundly surprise. Thwarting expectation, the surprising element may indeed provoke the revision of theory, even the reorganization of categories, thus producing novelty as a result. It is itself, however, never a mere matter of novelty, but always of conflict with prior belief. The concept of unexpectedness, it should be noted, is too weak to make this critical distinction, for it covers both the case of a feature that has simply not been anticipated, and that of a feature that has been positively ruled out by anticipation.[23]

To the extent that we are capable of surprise, the possibility that our expectations are wrong is alive for us and thus our joy in verification, if it occurs, is not utterly deluded. Receptive to surprise, we are capable of learning from experience—capable, that is, of acknowledging the inadequacies of our initial beliefs, and recognizing the need for their improvement. It is thus that the testing of theories, no less than their generation, calls upon appropriate emotional dispositions.

Receptivity to surprise involves, however, a certain vulnerability; it means accepting the risk of a possibly painful unsettlement of one's beliefs, with the attendant need to rework one's expectations and redirect one's conduct. To be sure, where the relevant beliefs are weakly held, or relatively segregated, or of peripheral significance for one's basic orientation—or where the required alterations are likely to be readily effected—the risk may be easily borne, even by the cautious. Surprise may, in such circumstances, not in fact distress but amuse—even enchant, as will be evident from even brief reflection on the role of surprise in humor, in music, in literature, and generally in the arts. Moreover, there are, in all realms of life, pleasant surprises, where the value of the unexpected event, or even of the unsettlement itself, outweighs the stress of disorientation and the concomitant costs of revision in belief.

One cannot, however, reasonably count on all—even most—surprises in life to be thus amusing or pleasant; it must be conceded that a general openness to surprise involves a real risk of epistemic distress. This risk may to varying degrees become palatable, even exciting; certainly accepting it is one of the normal requirements of rational character. Yet it is a risk of possibly painful disorientation, and it requires emotional strength to face and to master. To commit oneself to learning from experience is, in short, a significant attitude—supported by mature reflection, to be sure—but exacting a price in return for the prospect of improvement in one's system of beliefs.

Three alternative attitudes promise an avoidance of the price by erecting wholesale defenses against surprise. Since surprise presumes prior expectation, a defense may be sought, to begin with, in the rejection of all expectation—in effect, the denial of all belief. This is the attitude of the radical skeptic, who hopes to make himself immune to surprise by any contingency through renouncing all anticipations to the contrary, that is to say, all anticipations without exception. Of whatever happens, he says, in effect, "It doesn't surprise me since I never expected it not to happen!" A second—apparently opposite—attitude is that of utter credulity or gullibility—the acceptance of all beliefs or expectations without distinction. Here the formula in response to every contingency is "I'm not surprised! I expected that too!" Both radical skepticism and radical credulity are, however, alike forms of epistemic apathy: To reject all expectations is to be indifferent to each, while to accept all as equally good is in actuality to choose none, having no reason to expect anything at all rather than something else. It is no wonder that these seemingly contrary attitudes have so often been remarked to be psychologically akin, and together opposed to the selective hypothesis-formation characteristic of scientific thought. "Complete doubt," as Peirce noted, is "a mere self-deception" and no one who follows the method of radical skepticism "will ever be satisfied until he has formally recovered all those beliefs which in form he has given up."[24]

Moreover, each of these two alternative attitudes exacts its own heavy price. Neither can in fact be realized as a genuine option over a significant area of conduct. The skeptic, despite himself, forms positive expectations in executing his actions, while the radically credulous person, generally hospitable to inconsistencies, perforce rules out certain contingencies in carrying through the activities of daily life. Only in a local and intermittent way can these attitudes be attempted. They are perhaps more accurately described as poses or pretenses, the effect of which is, however, perfectly real—to aid the denial of responsibility for one's beliefs and so to block the possibility of their improvement through the educative medium of surprise.

The third attitude promising a defense against surprise is that of dogmatism. Unlike the radical skeptic and the total believer, the dogmatist is perfectly firm about the beliefs he espouses and the beliefs he rejects. He blocks surprise not by disclaiming responsibility for his doctrines, but rather by denying all experience that purports to contradict them. He not only avoids the systematic testing of his beliefs; he closes off the very possibility of recognizing negative evidence, by early and stout denial of its existence. Theory-laden to the point of blindness, his observations are predictably positive, the joy he takes in verification thus unearned and hollow. Dogmatism is also a difficult attitude to maintain if only because (as Peirce saw)[25] it is impossible to filter all negative indications in advance by a systematic method. Yet it can be carried a long way, preventing the acknowledgment of surprise, and, hence, the application of new and surprising experience to the improvement of initial beliefs and orientations. Dogmatism, no less than skepticism and gullibility, conflicts with the effort at such improvement. To accept this effort, with its associated vulnerability to the unsettlement of surprise, is to choose a distinctive emotional as well as cognitive path.

But how, it may be asked, is receptivity to surprise possible? Surprise is, after all, unsettling; it risks the distress of disorientation and the potential pain of relearning. In similar vein, Schlick contrasts the joy of verification with the disappointment of falsification[26]—the disappointment following upon the violation of beliefs in which we had put our trust. How can one counsel receptivity to surprise: Is this not an impossibly mixed emotion, like elation at despair, or happiness at depression?

We must, first of all, reject the suggestion that surprise is always painful. If Schlick's notion of uniformly joyful verification is to be rejected as extravagant, in line with our earlier remarks, his parallel notion of uniformly disappointing falsification must equally be criticized. Some falsifications are, as we have previously intimated, delightful, some disruptions of expectation pleasantly exciting, some occasions of relearning fraught with engaging challenge. Schlick, I suggest, confuses expectation with hope, but the two are clearly separable, and only the former is necessary for surprise.

Yet if surprise is not always painful, surely it sometimes is: It must therefore be conceded, at the very least, to be uncertain in its quality. The question then recurs in a new version: How can one counsel receptivity to uncertainty? Here, however, an immediate reply is forthcoming. The original version of the question raised the issue of impossibly mixed emotions, whereas the present version no longer does so. For uncertainty is not an emotion; it is rather a prospect or condition, while the feeling of uncertainty mixes readily with receptive and aversive attitudes. Uncertainty is indeed consistently faced in varying ways: Some persons tend to shrink from, while others tend to welcome the prospect. The receptivity to surprise that is implicated in the capacity to learn from experience is, in any case, perfectly coherent in its emotional composition.

Moreover, receptivity to surprise is not to be confused with elation or happiness. It is rather the capability of acknowledging surprise than joy in its occurrence that is here in point. Analogously, to acknowledge one's grief does not entail being elated by it. Acknowledgment itself is a possible and a significant attitude, opening the way beyond the acknowledged circumstance.

Yet receptivity is, of course, not enough to characterize the testing phase of inquiry. How we cope with surprise, once it is acknowledged, is of critical importance. Surprise may be dissipated and evaporate into lethargy. It may culminate in confusion or panic. It may be swiftly overcome by a redoubled dogmatism. Or it may be transformed into wonder or curiosity, and so become an educative occasion. Curiosity replaces the impact of surprise with the demand for explanation;[27] it turns confusion into question. To answer the question is to reconstruct initial beliefs so that they may consistently incorporate what had earlier been unassimilable. It is to provide an improved framework of premises by which the surprising event might have been anticipated and for which parallel events will no longer surprise.

Critical inquiry in pursuit of explanation is a constructive outcome of surprise, transforming initial disorientation into motivated search. There is, as we have seen, no mechanical routine that guarantees success in the search for explanatory theory. Yet, an emotional value of such search is to offer mature consolation for the stress of surprise and the renunciation of inadequate beliefs.[28] Achieving superordinate status in the economy of science, the value of inquiry becomes, indeed, autonomous, pressing new explanations deliberately into situations of risk, testing their vulnerability in novel ways, exposing their implicit predictions systematically to the chance of new surprise.

The constructive conquest of surprise is registered in the achievement of new explanatory structures, while cognitive application of these structures provokes surprise once more. Surprise is vanquished by theory, and theory is, in turn, overcome by surprise. Cognition is thus two-sided and has its own rhythm; it stabilizes and coordinates; it also unsettles and divides. It is responsible for shaping our patterned orientations to the future, but it must also be responsive to the insistent need to learn from the future. Establishing habits, it must stand ready to break them. Unlearning old ways of thought, it must also power the quest for new, and greater, expectations.[29] These stringent demands upon our cognitive processes also constitute stringent demands upon our emotional capacities. The growth of cognition is thus, in fact, inseparable from the education of the emotions.

Notes

1 For a discussion of this theme in the context of the history of American thought, see Morton White, *Science and Sentiment in America* (New York: Oxford University Press, 1972).

2 On this topic, see R. S. Peters, "Reason and Passion," in *Education and the Development of Reason*, R. F. Dearden, P. H. Hirst, and R. S. Peters, eds. (London: Routledge and Kegan Paul, 1972), especially the section on the rational passions, pp. 225–27. See also John Rawls, *A Theory of Justice* (Cambridge, MA: Harvard University Press, 1971), esp. sections 67, 73–75; P. Foot, "Moral Beliefs," *Proceedings of the Aristotelian Society*, 59, 1958–1959; and B.A.O. Williams, "Morality and the Emotions," in *Problems of the Self*, B.A.O. Williams, ed. (Cambridge, UK: Cambridge University Press, 1973). A significant recent book, dealing with a wide range of related topics, is Robert C. Solomon, *The Passions* (New York: Doubleday, Anchor Press, 1976).

3 Cp. Aristotle, *Nicomachean Ethics*, Book II, 3.

4 Peters, "Reason and Passion," p. 226.

5 John Dewey, *Human Nature and Conduct* (New York: Henry Holt, 1922, 1930), p. 196.

6 Ibid.

7 Related points are discussed in Peters, "Reason and Passion"; R. S. Peters, "The Education of the Emotions," in Dearden, Hirst, and Peters, *Education and the Development of Reason*; G. Pitcher, "Emotion," in Dearden, Hirst, and Peters, *Education and the Development of Reason*; and R. W. Hepburn, "The Arts and the Education of Feeling and Emotion," in Dearden, Hirst, and Peters, *Education and the Development of Reason*. See also the article W. P. Alston, "Emotion and Feeling," in *The Encyclopedia of Philosophy* (New York: Macmillan, 1967), vol. 2, pp. 479–86.

8 Henry David Aiken, "Some Notes Concerning the Aesthetic and the Cognitive," *Journal of Aesthetics and Art Criticism*, 13 (1955): 390–91.

9 Nelson Goodman, *Languages of Art* (Indianapolis: Bobbs-Merrill, 1968), p. 248.

10 Ibid., p. 251.

11 Albert Einstein, "Autobiographical Notes," trans. Paul Arthur Schilpp, in *Albert Einstein: Philosopher-Scientist*, P. A. Schilpp, ed. (New York: Tudor Publishing, 1949), p. 7. The passage is quoted in a discussion of these and related points in I. Scheffler, *Science and Subjectivity* (Indianapolis: Bobbs-Merrill, 1967), esp. ch. 4.

12 Carl G. Hempel, *Philosophy of Natural Science* (Englewood Cliffs, NJ: Prentice-Hall, 1966), p. 16.

13 Michael Polanyi, *Personal Knowledge* (New York: Harper & Row, 1958, 1962), pp. 134–35.

14 Dewey, *Human Nature and Conduct*, p. 192.

15 For discussion helpful in clarifying certain points in this section, I am grateful to Professors Eli Hirsch and Jonas Soltis.

16 Moritz Schlick, "Über das Fundament der Erkenntnis," *Erkenntnis*, vol. 4, 1934, translated by David Rynin as "The Foundation of Knowledge," in *Logical Positivism*, A. J. Ayer, ed. (New York: Free Press, 1959).

17 Schlick, "Über das Fundament der Erkenntnis," in Ayer, *Logical Positivism*, pp. 222–23. There is a general discussion of Schlick's paper in Scheffler, *Science and Subjectivity*, ch. 5.

18 Schlick, "Über das Fundament der Erkenntnis," in Ayer, *Logical Positivism*, p. 227.

19 Scheffler, *Science and Subjectivity*, p. 30.

20 Jerome S. Bruner, J. J. Goodnow, and G. A. Austin, *A Study of Thinking* (New York: John Wiley, 1956), p. 47.

21 See N. R. Hanson, *Patterns of Discovery* (Cambridge, UK: Cambridge University Press, 1958), pp. 18–19, and elsewhere. For a general discussion, see Scheffler, *Science and Subjectivity*, especially chs. 1 and 2.

22 Ibid., ch. 2.

23 On these points, there is disagreement among previous writers. For informative historical, as well as other material see M. M. Desai, "Surprise: A Historical and Experimental Study," *British Journal of Psychology Monograph Supplements*, no. 22, 1939; D. E. Berlyne, "Emotional Aspects of Learning," *Annual Review of Psychology*, 15 (1964), 115–42; and W. R. Charlesworth, "The Role of Surprise in Cognitive Development," in *Studies in Cognitive Development*, D. Elkind and J. H. Flaveli, eds. (New York: Oxford University Press, 1969). Although I agree with various points in these psychological papers (e.g., Charlesworth, pp. 270, 276), they tend to focus on individual behavior in a relatively local situation, whereas I tend to link surprise with failed prediction in the context of discussions in philosophy of science.

24 C. S. Peirce, "Some Consequences of Four Incapacities," in *Collected Papers of Charles Sanders Peirce*, Charles Hartshorne and Paul Weiss, eds., vol. 5 (Cambridge, MA: Harvard University Press, 1934), 5:264–65. See also Israel Scheffler, *Four Pragmatists* (London: Routledge & Kegan Paul, 1974), pp. 52–53, 69–70.

25 C. S. Peirce, "The Fixation of Belief," in Hartshorne and Weiss, *Collected Papers of Charles Sanders Peirce*, 5:382. See also a general discussion in Scheffler, *Four Pragmatists*, pp. 60ff.

26 Schlick, "Über das Fundament der Erkenntnis," in Ayer, *Logical Positivism*, p. 223.

27   On explanation generally, see Israel Scheffler, *Anatomy of Inquiry* (New York: Alfred A. Knopf, 1963), Part I; also Bobbs-Merrill edition, 1971. I here use the term in a very broad sense.

28   Interesting discussion of this sort of point and related psychological issues is contained in Fay H. Sawyier, "About Surprise" (Paper read to the annual meeting of the Western Division of the American Philosophical Association, St. Louis, Missouri, 1974). For a discussion of the pedagogical use of surprise in the teaching of mathematics see Stephen I. Brown, "Rationality, Irrationality and Surprise," *Mathematics Teaching: The Bulletin of The Association of Teachers of Mathematics*, no. 55, Summer 1971.

29   On related points, see the papers by H. Gardner, M. W. Wartofsky, and N. Goodman in *The Monist*, 58 (1974): 319–42.

Index

abduction, 24, 47
access to truth, 8–9, 32
    indirect, 18
    as metaphor, 17–18
act-incompatibility, 121
actions
    incongruity of, 120, 121
    justification of, 114
    significance of, and agent's
        responsibility, 118
    systematic import of, 122
aesthetic experience, 129–30
aesthetic judgments, sentences
        containing, 44
affirmation, 43, 44
agency, and responsibility, 118. *See
    also* actions
agreement
    with reality, 62
    ultimate, and truth here and now,
        56
Aiken, H. D., 129–30
apathy, epistemic, 137
approximation, 64
a priori method, in inquiry, 104, 105
Aristotle
    on terrestrial *vs.* celestial motion, 47
    on truth, 39
art
    and perceptive emotion, 129–30

and reenactment, 88
and ritual, 84, 85–86
    sentimentalized, 125
Atkinson, J. W., 17
attributions, fallibility of, 43
Austin, G. A., 134
authority, as method in inquiry, 104,
    105
axiom, 23–24
Ayer, A. J., 76

Bain, Alexander, 102, 103
beliefs, 7–8
    certainty of, precluded, 102
    clusters of, 72
    fixation of, 104
    and linearity, 20
    Peirce on doubt and, 21–22
    prior to doubt, 106
    surprisingly disconfirmed, 136
benzene ring, and Kekulé's snakes,
    131
Bergson, Henri, 88
Bonjour, Laurence, 8
brain dead, utterances by the, 9
Bruner, Jerome, 134

cable metaphor, Peirce's, 2, 24, 48
Cambridge pragmatists, 96
Cantril, H., 17

Carnap, Rudolf, 41–42, 58, 62
Cassirer, Ernst, 82–83, 83–84, 85, 86,
    88
censorship, 105
certainty
    based on meaning, 1
    conviction of, and dogmatism, 33
    and elimination of endless
        regress, 18
    mathematical, 11–12
    of own existence, *see* "Cogito ergo
        sum" argument
    and philosophy, 2
    quest for, as end to inquiry, 1
    and truth, 32, 42–44
    unattainability of, 100, 102
character, rational, 127
Chomsky, Noam, 70–71
circularity, 25
    wide, 26
clusters, 50–51
    commonalities among, without
        reduction, 80
    in science, 52–53, 72, 89
co-exemplification, 87
"Cogito ergo sum," 9
    vulnerability of, 9–11
cognition. *See also* thought
    emotions in the service of, 125–32
    in ethical judgments, 119
    growth of, 139
    as a variety of action, 119
cognitive emotions, 132–39
cognitive theorists, 44
Cohen, Morris R., 26
coherence, 116
    justification for rules of, 117
community, conception of, and
        reenactment, 88
conception, as "teleological
        instrument," 100. *See also*
        symbolism

confirmation, 34–35
    vs. absolute truth, 41–42
consciousness
    and doubt, 106
    religious, 88
continuity
    of ends and means, 80
    vs. dualisms, 99
controls, democratic, in justification,
    25–27
convention, 19
convergence, scientific, *vs.* revolution,
    65–66
conviction of certainty, and
    dogmatism, 33
credibility
    complete and permanent, 57
    initial, 15, 20–21, 47, 115–16, 117,
        120
    intrinsic, 15
    maximization of, 117
    of self-referential assertions, 11
    total, of system, 116, 118
credulity, radical, 137
crises in science, 51–52
crucial experiments, falsifying, 116
curiosity, 139

decision, 19
decree, 19–20
democratic controls, in justification,
    25–27
democratic society, pragmatism's
    model of, 101
denotation in ritual, 81, 83, 84
Descartes, René, 9, 13, 102
Dewey, John, 22, 80, 98
    on education, 111
    on emotional response to objects,
        132
    ethical naturalism, 79–81
    and the habit of intelligence, 97

Hegelian traits in, 96
on the nature of problems, 103
on rationality, 127–28
on shared experience, 101
on symbols, 100
"warranted assertibility," 56
dialectical response to reduction
    failure, 49
dictionaries, wide circularity in, 26
discourse-dependence, 61. *See also*
    version-dependence
diversity, biological, over time, 90n.34
dogmatism, 19, 137–38
    and conviction of certainty, 33
    serial, 20
domains. *See also* worlds
    corresponding to credible versions,
        70
    multiple and unreduced, 67
    of points and lines, 69
    scientific, 71
doubt
    feigned, Peirce's, *see* "feigned
        hesitancy"
    Peirce on, 21–22, 102
    provocative of inquiry, 102, 104,
        107 (*see also* doubt-belief
        theory of inquiry)
    radical, 2, 102, 103, 108
    scientific, 109
doubt-belief theory of inquiry,
    Peirce's, 56–57, 102–6
    difficulties in, 106–8
dreams, and myth, 83
Dyson, Freeman, 74

Einstein, Albert, 131
eliminatist instrumentalism, 46
emotions
    cognitive, 125–26, 132–39
    education of, 139
    and perception, 128–30

emotive theories of ethics, 44,
    75–77
empirical "checkpoints," 78
empirical sciences
    and access to truth, 32 (*see also*
        science)
    justification in, 23–25
empiricism
    of C. I. Lewis, 14–17
    and justification, 8–9
ends and means, continuity of, 80
epistemic apathy, 137
equilibrium, reflective, 27
ethics
    cognitive nature of judgment in,
        119
    emotive theories of, 44, 75–77
    and false dichotomy of emotion
        and cognition, 125
    justification in, 2, 114
    naturalism, 79–81
    reducibility to science, 76, 77, 79
    sentences using terms of, 44
    subjectivity in, 123
Euclidean geometry, 11–12
evidence
    and "Cogito" utterances, 10–11
    in science, 1
evolution, 72, 90n.34, 98
    human, perceptive emotion in,
        128
    theory of, 24
excluded middle, 34
exemplification, ritual, 81, 84, 85, 88
expansive moment, in scientific
    inquiry, 52, 72, 74, 80
experience
    aesthetic, 129–30
    shared, 101
experiments, crucial, and changes in
    initial credibility, 116
expression, as form of reference, 84

fact, correspondence with, 115
fallibilism, 56, 99, 100, 102
falsification
   and delight, 138
   of scientific hypotheses, 48
fantasy, and myth, 83
fear of a particular person, 128–29
features
   expressed in ritual, cognition of, 86
   unanticipated *vs.* ruled out in
     advance, 136
feelings. *See also* emotions; passions
   denotation of, in ritual, 83
   perceptive, 128–30
Feigl, Herbert, 50
"feigned hesitancy," Peirce's, 107,
    107–8, 109
Fisch, Max, 98
fixity and truth, 36–38
frames of reference, indispensability
   of, 68
Fries, J. F., 19, 28n.18
functional view of thought, 100

Galileo, dropping of iron balls by, 35,
   36
games, 12
gases, kinetic theory of, 48
geometry, Euclidean, certainty in,
   11–12
gestures
   as communication of meaning, 96
   mimetic, 87
   ritual, 85
given, the, in Lewis' empiricism, 14–16

Gombrich, Ernst, 16
"good," definability of, 77. *See also*
   "wrong"
Goodman, Nelson, 4
   on apprehending art, 130
   associates arts and sciences, 81

expands definition of reference, 84
   on expression and exemplification,
     85–86
   on induction, 27
   and initial credibility, 15, 20–21,
     115
   irrealism, 66–70
   on total credibility, 57
   version-dependent pluralism,
     59–61, 62
Goodnow, J. J., 134
groundedness, *vs.* justification,
    118–19
growth
   facts of, 90n.34
   rapid personal, 122
gullibility, 137

habits
   belief-related, 107
   of intelligence, 97
Hume, David, 79
hypocrisy, 85, 86–87

idealism, 14, 55
   Lewis' critique of, 14–17
identity theory, mind-body, 50
imagination
   objects of, and problem-solving,
     132
   theoretical, 130–32
     (*see also* art; myth; religion)
incompatibility
   of acts, 120
   of competing systems, 115, 117
indignation, 132
individualism
   abandoned as epistemic ideal, 100
   methodological, 48, 70
indoctrination, 105
induction, Goodman's justification
   of, 27

infinite regress
  avoidance of, 18, 19
  and relativization of truth, 31, 32
initial credibility, 15, 20–21, 47, 115–
    16, 117, 120
inquiry
  emotional value of, 139
  end of, quest for certainty as, 1
  methods of, 104–6
  Peirce's doubt-belief theory of,
    see doubt-belief theory of
    inquiry
  scientific, expansion in, 52, 72, 74,
    80
  scientific, reduction in, 51, 52–53,
    63–64, 73, 74, 80
  stimulated by doubt, 102, 103, 104
instrumentalism, in the sciences,
    45–46
interactionism, vii, 27, 30
interconnection, 47
intrinsic credibility, 15
intuition, 102
intuitionism, ethical, 77–78
irrationality, *vs.* subjectivity, 123
irrealism, ix, 60, 66–70, 73

James, William, 22, 62, 73
  on conception as "teleological
    instrument," 100
  and the individual agent, 96, 97
  on the mutability of truth, 32, 35–
    36, 56
  on personal consistency, 120
joy of verification, 133–35
justification
  of actions, 114
  contextual and comparative, 22–23
  democratic controls in, 25–27
  in the empirical sciences, 23–25
  empiricist model of, 8–9
  ethico-legal, 2, 114, 120

and initial credibility, 21
interactional view of, 30
non-affirmational, 120, 122
rational and systematic structuring
    of, 122
rationalist model of, 8
and responsible behavior, 117–18
for rules of coherence, 117
in science, 2
of sentence-acceptance, 118
vs. access to truth, 18
vs. groundedness, 118–19

Kant, Immanuel, 96
Kekulé, F. A., 131
Kennedy, Gail, 98
kinetic theory of gases, 48
knowledge, foundational view of, 1.
    See also truth
Kuhn, Thomas S., 65–66

Langer, Susanne, 82, 83, 85, 86
Lewis, C. I., 14–17, 62, 115
Liar's paradox, 31, 58
limits, and the infinitesimal, 45
linearity, 19, 20, 23, 30
  vs. circularity, 25
linguistics irreducible to physics, 64,
    71
Locke, John, 102
logic, 12, 112
  classical, 12–14
  deviant, 14
  mathematics reduced to, 47
logical positivism, 56
  and "agreement with reality," 62

"magnetism" of moral language, 78
mathematics
  proof in, 23
  reduced to logic, 47
McClelland, D. C., 17

Mead, George Herbert, 96, 97
meaning, certainty based on, 1
method
    primacy of, 109–12
    scientific, 111
mind-body identity theory, 50
monism, ix, 62, 63–64, 73
    Peirce's modified, 64
Moore, G. E., 77–78
moral emotions, 132
moral language, "magnetism" of,
    78
moral terms, in sentences, 44
Murphey, Murray G., 96, 103
myth
    and dream, 83
    and fantasy, 83
    and ritual, 82–83

Nagel, Ernest, 26, 48
naturalism, ethical, 79–80
Neurath, Otto, 2, 56
normative ethics, and justification,
    114

objectivity without certainty, 3
objects, diverse, reference to, in
    ritual, 84
observations, theory-laden, 134–35,
    137
ontological reduction, 49
operationism and truth, 57–59
opinion, progressive change of, in
    science, 110

passions
    rational, 127–28
    scientific, 131–32
Peirce, Charles Sanders, 7
    and abduction, 24, 47
    and "agreement with reality," 62
    cable metaphor, 24, 48

and the development of
    pragmatism, 96–97
on doubt, 21–22
doubt-belief theory, 56–57, 102–6
on explanatory inadequacy of
    mechanical forces, 90n.34
and fallibilism, 56
on liberal education, 112
on methods in inquiry, 104–6,
    109–10
on radical doubt, 137
science-as-cable metaphor, 2
and semeiotic, 81
perception, role of emotions in,
    128–30
performance of ritual, as
    exemplification, 85, 88
Peters, R. S., 87, 88, 127
philosophy, nature of, 2–3
physicalism, ix, 48, 49
    "monopolistic," 72, 74
physics
    alleged primacy of, 64, 66, 74
    linguistics irreducible to, 64, 71
    unified field theory, 51, 72–73
pleasant surprises, 136
pluralism, 62
    in philosophy, 3
    versional, ix
    and worldmaking, 66 (*see also*
        version-dependence)
plurealism, ix, 62, 67, 68, 69, 74
Polanyi, Michael, 131–32
Popper, Karl R., 2, 19, 28n.18, 50
pragmatism, 21
    and "agreement with reality," 62
    and analytic methods, 3–4
    origins of, 95–98
    Quine's, 27
    responses to problems of, 99–102
    in the sciences, 45–46
    and symbolism, 81

predicate
    as legitimate scientific term, 43
    truth, 58
Principia Mathematica (Whitehead
        and Russell), 12, 47
principle of least action, 122
probability
    no guarantee of credibility, 115
    in science, 1, 99
problem situations, and ethical
        reasoning, 79–80
problem-solving, emotions in, 132
progressive change, in science, 110
proof, mathematical, 23. *See also*
        justification
provisionality and truth, 32–34
psychologism, 19, 28n.18
psychology, reduction of social
        sciences to, 70–71
pure mathematics, 12

Quine, W. V., 27
    on attribution of truth, 41
    empirical "checkpoints," 78
    and the Liar's paradox, 31
    on "nearer than," 65
    "nearer than" undefined for
        theories, 110
    on Tarski's semantic criterion, 55

rationalism
    and justification, 8
    vulnerability of "Cogito" argument,
        9–11
rationality, 123, 127–28
rational passions, 127–28
Rawls, John, 27
realism, 55, 63
reality, "agreement with," 62
reduction, 47–50
    and the alleged primacy of physics,
        66

as desideratum of science, 51, 63–
        64, 73
    failures in, 48–49
    limits on, 70–72
    and monism, 64
    of social sciences to psychology,
        70–71
reductive moment, 52–53, 74, 80
reenactment, in ritual, 81, 87–88, 88
reference
    in art and ritual, 84
    problems of, and ethico-legal
        justification, 120
reflective equilibrium, 27
relativism, radical, 60, 73
relativization, and infinite regress, 31
religion
    and false dichotomy of emotion and
        cognition, 125
    personal and institutional, 82
    primitive, stabilization in, 88
religious consciousness, 88
religious feeling, 83
remorse, 132
repetition, ritual, 81, 86, 87
responsibility, denial of, for one's
        beliefs, 137
responsible behavior, and justification,
        117–18
rightness, 57
ritual
    and art, 85–86
    cognition of expressed features,
        86
    gestures of, 85
    and myth, 82–83
    Parliamentary, 88
    repetition in, 86, 87
    sacrificial, 85
    symbolic function of, 81
rule-acceptance, and justification,
        117

Russell, Bertrand, 51
  and "intrinsic credibility," 15
  on postulation, 20

sacrifice, ritual, 85
schemata, *vs.* sentences, 37–38
Schlick, Moritz, 56, 62, 133, 134, 138
science
  and access to truth, 32
  alleged primacy of physics in, 64,
    66, 74
  "analytic" *vs.* "synthetic," 74
  and the arts, in Goodman, 81
  change of opinion progressive in,
    110
  clusters in, 51, 52–53
  confirmation of theories in, 34–35
  crises in, 51–52
  domains within, 70–71
  expansive *vs.* reductive moments in,
    72, 74, 80
  falsification of hypotheses in, 48
  justification in, 23–25
  Kuhn's model of revolutions,
    65–66
  method of, in inquiry, 104, 111
  nature of, 1–2
  objectivity precluding wishful
    thinking, 130
  reducibility of ethics to, 76, 77, 79
  reduction as desideratum of, 63–64,
    73
  self-correctiveness of, 101
  social conception of, 100
  systems in, 46–47
  theoretical terms within, 44–45
  validity of predicates in, 43
scientific imagination, 130–32
selfhood, in industrial society, 99–100
self-referential assertions, 10–11
Sellars, Wilfrid, 50
semantic criterion of truth, Tarski's,
  39–41, 55, 58, 61

semeiotic, 81, 102
semiotics. *See* semeiotic
sensations, 102
senses, trustworthiness of, 13. *See also*
  empiricism
"sensuously given," the, 14–16
sentence-acceptance, justification of,
  118
sentences
apparent indicative, and skepticism,
  45
  hybrid ethical, 76–77
  initial credibility of, 115–16, 117,
    120
  as truth candidates, 44
  vs. schemata, 37–38
set theory, 12, 47
Sherif, M., 17
simplicity, 47. *See also* reduction
simplification, 52
skepticism
  and apparent indicative sentences,
    45
  radical, 109, 136–37
stability
  in primitive religion, 88
  through flexibility, in science,
    111
  through intellectual method,
    100–101
standard act-set, 122
statistical mechanics, thermodynamics
  reduced to, 48
Stevenson, C. L., 76, 78
string theories, 51, 73
subjectivism, *vs.* relativity, 3
subjectivity, *vs.* irrationality, 123
surprise, 135–36
  defenses against, 136–38
  receptivity to, 138–39
symbols
  and ritual, 81, 83
  worlds without, 68

systems
  formal, interpreted *vs.*
    uninterpreted, 11–12
  incompatible, 115
  justification for accepting, 115–17
  in science, 46–47

Tarski, Alfred, 39–41, 55
tenacity, as method of inquiry, 104–5
test, in science, 1. *See also* crucial
    experiment
theoretical terms, within science,
    44–45
theory
  of everything, 51, 52–53, 64, 72–75
  relationship of observation to, 1
thermodynamics, reduced to statistical
    mechanics, 48
thought
  constrained by external data, 62
  pragmatism's functional view of, 100
  as sign, 102
threat, perception of, 128–29
token production, 61
total credibility, of system, 116
transparency of truth, 38–42
trustworthiness of the senses, 13
truth
  absolute, ix, 37
  access to, *see* access to truth
  attribution of, 41
  and certainty, 32, 41, 42–44
  consistent with pluralism, 3
  eligibility of apparent indicative
    sentences, 45
  and emotive theories of ethics,
    75–77
  estimation of, 43
  and fixity, 36–38
  here and now, *vs.* ultimate
    agreement, 56
  import of, *vs.* estimation of, 32, 33
  and operationism, 57–59

  philosophies of, 55–57
  and provisionality, 32–34
  Tarski's "semantic criterion" of,
    39–41, 55, 58, 61
  transparency of, 38–42
  variability, and estimation of, 35
  vs. complete and permanent
    credibility, 57
  vs. confirmation, 41–42
  vs. verification, 34–36
truth predicate, 58

unexpectedness, 135–36
uninterpreted sentences, 12

verification
  joy of, 133–35
  vs. truth, 34–36
verificationism, ix
version-dependence, 59–61, 70
voluntarism, 19–20

"warranted assertibility," Dewey's, 56
Weierstrass, Karl, 45
White, Morton, 27
wishful thinking, 125, 130
wonder, 139
words, worlds without, 68
worldmaking
  and Goodman's "features," 61
  as metaphor for version-making, 67
    (*see also* version-dependency)
worlds. *See also* domains
  conflicting, 57, 59
  corresponding to credible versions,
    70
  version-dependence of, 59–61
world-versions, 70. *See also* systems;
    version-dependence
  disparate, and conflicting worlds, 59
"wrong" as cognate of "Bah" or
    "Humbug," 76
Wundt, Wilhelm, 96